DISCOVER THE BEST IN YOUR

RELATIONSHIPS

Life Coaching *for* Muslims

Sayeda Habib

Discover the Best in Your Relationships: Life Coaching for Muslims
First Published in England by
Kube Publishing Ltd
MCC, Ratby Lane, Markfield
Leicestershire, LE67 9SY
United Kingdom

Tel: +44 (0) 1530 249230
Website: www.kubepublishing.com
Email: info@kubepublishing.com

A cataloguing-in-publication data record of this book
is available from the British Library.

ISBN: 978-1-84774-163-9
eISBN: 978-1-84774-164-6

Cover Design: Nasir Cadir
Concept Design: Imtiaze Ahmed
Typesetting: Nasir Cadir
Printed by: Elma Basim, Turkey

Contents

DEDICATION

In the name of God, Most Merciful, Most Compassionate.

I dedicate this book to all human beings who are challenging themselves, making changes, and striving towards improving an important relationship.

I hope that this book will bring you comfort through the tough times, and, be a valuable asset on your journey to more fulfilling relationships and greater inner peace.

Acknowledgements

First of all, I am grateful to my Creator for giving me the opportunity to serve my community through this book. I feel truly blessed to be doing such fulfilling work. With that said, a big thank you to all of my clients for your trust, for sharing your stories, and allowing me to support you along your journey. Specifically, thanks to Ambreen Saleh for reading the early chapters and giving feedback, and to Ali Ahsani for jumping in at a moment's notice to help me with the Hadith selections. To my friends and colleagues, thank you so much for your moral support, it really helps me stay focused on the bigger picture. And last, but definitely not the least, a big thank you to my husband Sabir Ali, for pushing me to grow, and giving me the space to do what I love. To my darling Zainab – thank you for giving me the joy of being your mom – and for challenging me to show up as a better human being every day.

Foreword

Dear fellow explorer,

As salaamu alaykum. How are you? I am curious about what prompted you to pick up this specific book. Perhaps you have read my first book, *Discover the Best in You* and found it beneficial, *masha'Allah*?

My first book was designed to offer coaching and help you gain some insight into various aspects of your life, such as goal setting, creating abundance, enhancing self-care and managing your time. Although it did touch on relationships a little, this second book, *Discover the Best in Your Relationships*, is a more specific and in-depth look at the important relationships in our lives. I personally feel that the quality of one's relationships impacts upon a person's human experience more than anything else. When a relationship isn't working in my life, it can impact how I feel about everything else. So, if you also feel that way, rest assured that you're not on your own. Think back to when you were dealing with a challenge at work, or with health etc; who or what helped you get through it? Did your relationships offer you strength? Or did a certain relationship make it even harder to get through that challenge?

This book is a deep-dive into how human beings "do" relationships. You will learn some concepts that are important for relationships in general. Next, this book will help you explore a specific relationship that you wish to improve. Most of the relationships that impact our lives on a daily basis are covered here. Do keep in mind that some of these principles can be applied to relationships that have not been directly mentioned. As with the previous book, you can read the chapters that are relevant to you. However, I do recommend that you read the first two chapters before diving in to the others. These two chapters give you the foundations upon which the rest of the book rests. After that, select the chapters that you feel are most relevant to your life right now and go from there.

What can you expect from this journey? As with the previous book, I invite you to work with this book just as you would in person with a life coach. Coaching is a process that helps you go from where you are to where you truly want to be. It's a process based on gentle inquiry and it's designed to provide a safe, non-judgemental space where you, the client, can truly explore how to enhance a specific area of your life. Coaching does require some work – it is not a process that's done *to* you. In fact, it's a process that you fully engage with at every step. When you are "coachable", you will discover things that you really love about yourself, and you will gain some personal insights about that which may challenge you as well. I trust that if you approach this book with an open mind, and with a willingness to coach yourself, you will make productive changes that stay with you for the long term. If you would like to know more about life coaching, please refer to the first chapter in my previous book, *Discover the Best in You*.

As you start to reflect and explore, imagine that I am present, sitting with you and asking you the questions. Imagine that you are working with me in the comfort of your own space, and at your own pace. Get yourself a coaching journal and keep track of all your work in this one place. This way you will be able to refer to your insights and map them across to different relationships. Take your time, and remember that the real outcome is growth, and creating the changes you want. There have been many times when clients will take time with a certain area, and that's okay. There is no hurry, no judgement, and nothing to prove. You may want a relationship to change very quickly, but remember that changes can take time. Be honest, but compassionate with yourself as you navigate through this journey.

I hope that you will find this book useful for years to come. The natures of our relationships change as we go through various different stages of life. Keep coming back to these exercises in due course as you continue on your journey towards greater fulfilment. I wish you all the best on your journey.

Finally, I would like to draw your attention to the fact that the client's stories mentioned in this book are real, but names have been changed to protect individual identities.

Sayeda Habib
Chicago, ILLINOIS.
USA
June 1, 2021

1.

What is a Relationship?

It is He who creates human beings from fluid,
then makes them kin by blood and marriage:
your Lord is all powerful.

Qur'an 25: 54

'Verily one of the good deeds to be rewarded the fastest is reconciliation with one's kin.'

Prophet Muhammad (pbuh)

What is a relationship? This may sound like a very simple question, but start to answer it and it may become more complicated than you first thought. Let's test this idea. Put pen to paper and fill in the following:

I think that a relationship is ______________________________

____

Use the statement above as your starting point. This is your general definition of what a relationship is. Now let's build on this definition. Reflect on the impact that one of your relationships currently has on you. How do you feel as you think about this person? Does it feel good, or bad being in relationship with him or her? Our relationships impact our lives in the most profound ways, don't they? Some of them may be full of joy, while others are incredibly difficult.

Our experiences within a certain relationship may shape our views about all of our relationships. We may do this without even realizing. Below is a list of some concepts that can be applied to relationships in general. Take a moment to reflect on the following, and choose whichever ones apply to you. Be frank and open with yourself; think about the variety of relationships in your life and then choose from the list below.

A relationship is:

- A bond you choose.
- Destined; not actively chosen.
- A connection with another that allows room for both to grow and be nurtured in one way or another.

- Riddled with obligations; things you have to do.
- Hard work.
- Full of compromise and giving in.
- An opportunity to experience joy and connection.

Now take a moment to write down what you believe are the three most important facets of any relationship.

In my opinion, the three most important characteristics of any relationship are:

____

____

____

You will have now gotten some conscious awareness of how you're thinking about relationships in general. As you reflect, feel free to jot down any other important characteristics that come to mind. Each person will have his or her own definition of what a relationship is/should be, because we have all been through unique experiences. Your relationships with parents, siblings, even your community will shape your view of how you think about relationships now.

As you embark on this journey to creating more fulfilling relationships, remind yourself that your attitude about your relationships will directly impact how fulfilled you feel within them. Even though it's natural for most of us to experience one or two difficult relationships, if you think that relationships, in general, are hard work and full of compromise, they definitely will be. We cannot but manifest what we believe to be true. Whether you're very positive, or feeling a little negatively about a certain relationship right now, take some time to work on the exercise below, as it will be your starting point for your work through this book. The exercise is designed to increase your own awareness of how you experience your relationships and it will provide you with valuable information that will guide you from here on out.

Exercise 1.1: Basic Relationship Audit: Exploring Your Motivation To Change...

The aim of this exercise is to support you in exploring your general view of relationships. This information will be invaluable, especially if most of your relationships are currently strained.

Method of the exercise: Take your journal, label the exercise, and answer the questions below:

Part A: General awareness:

1. On a scale from one to 10, How fulfilled am I in my relationships?
2. What do I see, feel, hear or experience that tells me that I am at this number?
3. How are my relationships impacting the quality of my life right now?

Part B: Specific awareness:

1. Which one relationship in my life is particularly challenging right now?
2. What will my life be like in the next 5–10 years, if this relationship stays the way it is now? Is this OK with me?
3. How will my life change if this relationship were to be better?
4. On a scale from 1–10, how willing am I now to work towards improving this relationship?
5. Am I willing to take action, even if the other person does not know or do anything different?

Note: Scales will always go from 1–10. One being the least, and ten being the most of the concept or criterion being discussed. So in this example, you would score ten if you are 100% motivated to improve this relationship.

The above exercise should have tested your motivation to change a specific relationship in your life. *To be motivated means that one is ready to move and to take action towards a particular goal.* Many times, we might tell ourselves that we really wish to change something, but we don't do anything about it. This essentially means that we like the idea of it, but that goal isn't really one of our top priorities. This probably sounds harsh, but I'm sure you yourself can look back and notice the things that you really took action on, and the ones you didn't. The areas where you took action, and still do, are the current priorities. There may be other areas that you would like to improve, but they haven't made it to the top of the list yet. There's nothing wrong with this, it is just something to notice.

Life involves a lot of juggling most of the time. Often, we just let our relationships remain the way they are because we don't have the time or the energy to invest into shifting them. This might be all right for the short term, but let's remember that the quality of our lives does depend on the quality of our relationships. Think about that one relationship you just explored earlier. How do you feel each time you think about this person? How do these feelings impact your health, your state of mind, and your overall ability to be productive? If this relationship is an important one, then you might well find yourself suffering along with the relationship.

The above exercise asked you to look at how this challenging relationship will impact your life. If it is impacting your life now, chances are it will continue doing so if things don't change. Ask yourself: *"is it ok for me to keep suffering this way?"* If you are now able to state that it's not acceptable for things to stay this way, then you have the motivation to do something about it. Well done to you if you have now reached this point; this motivation will carry you through your journey.

"Relationship" defined

Each relationship in our life has its own unique meaning, obligations, and rewards. That being said, we will still aim to define what a relationship "should be" in general terms. The reason for a definition is to provide us with an overall context to work from. Once you begin to use this definition as an overall foundation, then you can choose to shape a definition for each specific relationship in your life as you work through this book.

In my first book *Discover the Best in You* we defined a relationship as *A bond that is created when people choose to pay attention to, communicate with, or connect with someone else. (p. 110)*

If you look at how we talk about relationships here, you will notice that we refer to it as a "created" bond. This definition will apply to all ties, including those that we have by birth. We may be tied to people by birth, but that doesn't mean that we necessarily have a bond with them. We as Muslims know the importance of maintaining ties with blood relations so it brings us back to the very concept that we are referring to here – that all our relationships become "relationships by choice". A relationship starts taking shape when we choose to connect with another human being with an aim or a goal. That goal could be companionship, sharing, working towards a business, or even creating a family together. Whatever the desired outcome, it's that choice that keeps us working towards it.

So our more complete definition of what a relationship is goes as follows:

The bond that is created between people when they choose to connect with one another in order to achieve a common goal, or to enhance the potential in each other.

What's the first thing that you reacted to in this statement? Was it that a relationship could be about enhancing potential, or that a relationship is a choice? The word "relationship" is so commonly used that we don't really reflect on whether they are by choice or not. It has become a generic word for all our ties. However, I now invite you to use it differently. Take pen to paper, and make two columns. Label one column as "Ties I'm nurturing". Label the other as "Ties that are suffering/ not being nurtured". List those connections that you are currently nurturing (and enjoying) as "relationships". Next, use the second column to list the relationships that are suffering, or being neglected.

Any relationship that's suffering hardly feels like a choice, and it can cloud how we experience all our other relationships, where no relationship feels like a choice. You are justified in feeling this way. A relationship that is suffering will not feel like a choice. As painful as it is, think about it as a connection of birth or circumstance right now, but keep the intention that you will work towards transforming it into a fulfilling relationship.

It may seem like a lot of work to transform a relationship, and it may well be. But remember, leaving it as it is will have a negative impact on your life in the long run. Maintain the hope that things will get better and indeed this will be a fulfilling journey. You may well experience the transformation of this relationship. How is that possible? By transforming your own thought and behaviour: the chapters in this book are aimed at supporting you in doing just that, insha' Allah.

Setting the foundation for fulfilling relationships

How might we improve a suffering "relationship"? We have talked about any relationship being a connection of choice, but it is important to remember that each tie will have its own unique requirements. However, there are some general principles pertaining to all ties and relationships as a whole. When we apply these principles, they can help us enhance how we experience all our connections. These principles may also support us, as individuals, to feel more fulfilled within. Think of these principles as setting a foundation for each relationship that's already in our life, or yet to come. Understand each principle so that it becomes easier to understand and apply it. Of course, you can choose the ones you wish to apply (or not). Note that these are general principles that will apply to most of our relationships. At times, there may be exceptions where a person may be suffering in an abusive relationship, or in a relationship with someone suffering from mental illness. These principles may not apply then. The idea here is to use these principles as a general guideline that will help us to shift our paradigm so we can enhance our relationships. That being said, now let's look at what they are:

1. Each human being does his or her best given the circumstances

You know you are giving things your best shot, remember that the other person is doing the same. He or she is working with the resources they have and doing the best they can.

Example: Your spouse has become unemployed. He or she is at home practically all the time. It seems that s/he isn't doing much to change the situation. Remember that it may appear like this on the outside, but consider the idea that this person is doing their very best, given the challenges that they have been dealt.

2. Each human being has the same inherent need for being loved, cherished and respected

As you appreciate being shown respect or love, the other person does too. Give it wholeheartedly before you expect to receive it.

Tip: Let's say that someone in your life is being disrespectful to you. Put yourself in their shoes for a while and try to figure out what love or respect means to them. Go ahead and aim to be this way, for a while, and see if something begins to shift.

3. We need to deal with conflicts in a respectful manner

Conflicts will happen and there will be disagreement. This however, does not excuse anger, sarcasm, or putting another person down. Speak with them as you wish to be spoken to.

Example: Think of the last time when you either had an angry outburst or used sarcasm during a conflict. Ask the other person (even if it's your child) how it felt to be on the receiving end. Getting some feedback on how it feels to the other person will be the awareness required for change. Remember, if you speak in this manner, you might well get a similar type of response. Model how you wish to be spoken to and you are more likely to get a similar response.

4. Each behaviour, even if it impacts others in a negative way, meets an important need for the person carrying out that behaviour

When someone you are close to does something that annoys or hurts you, remember that is not their intent to do so. They are merely aiming to meet a need they have even though they may not be doing it in the best or even most considerate way. Keeping this in mind may prevent you from taking their behaviour personally and will make finding a solution much easier.

Example: Someone in your family is a smoker and the smoke is extremely uncomfortable and annoying for you. Keep in mind that the intention of this person is not to annoy you; instead it is to meet the need of the addiction. The smoking habit will also have a deeper, more fundamental need underneath.

5. Accept that disappointments will happen

Each human being has some flaws. Remember that there may be times when your loved ones may not meet your expectations. This is just their humanity. Remember the times when you didn't meet theirs?

Example: Think back to a time when someone asked you for a favour and you agreed to do it. You even gave it a good go, but things didn't work out. Sometimes we end up disappointing those we love despite our best intentions. The next time a loved one disappoints you, think about it from a different perspective. Remember their humanity, and yours! This way you'll be able to forgive more easily and maintain the relationship.

6. Have conversations, not confrontations

Confronting someone with an issue will only make the other person defensive. Bring the problem up with empathy and respect; they are more likely to listen and work with you.

Example: If you have ever had a shouting match with someone, then that is a confrontation, not a conversation. Think about how the "conversation" ended. Was anything resolved in a positive way, or did it leave you both feeling upset? Confrontations will leave each person with a bitter taste in their mouth. The next time an issue arises where things are starting to escalate, move away immediately. Respectfully get some space, take a deep breath. Use the time to make some notes about the concern, and aim towards a calm and collected conversation later on.

7. Aim to fix the situation, NOT the person

Talk about the situation or behaviour that bothers you. Keep the person's identity out of it; after all, they are in your life for good reason. Keep the big picture in mind...

Example: You hear two people arguing. Each one is saying, "you are like this, and you're like that" using blameful words and shouting at one another. Each time we talk about a person's character, we are damaging our own bond with them. Focus on using "I" language, gently talking about the behaviour that you did not like. You are more likely to get a better response.

8. Be prepared to be vulnerable

Sharing how we truly feel may be the scariest thing ever, but that's the one thing that brings us closer together than any other.

Tip: Be open to saying "I love you" but only when you mean it. Remember there's always the fear that someone might hurt you, but more often than not, the ones who are close to you really want to know what you feel and what's going on for you. Share, and experience the connection!

9. Know the difference between a request and a demand

A request is asking someone to do something when they have a choice to say no. A demand is when there's no choice given. Know the difference. Demands are best used sparingly.

Example: How do you know the difference between a request and a demand? Think about the last time someone asked you for something, but you knew that you couldn't say no to him or her because they would have a tantrum or get upset. This means that it wasn't a request at all, it was something you just had to do. In the same way, when you make a "request" of someone, ensure that you can be ok with it, if they tell you that they can't do it. If not, then tell them that you "need" it done.

10. Be eager to forgive, and open to apology

If you have done something to hurt the other person, apologize sincerely, and be eager to forgive if you've been asked. Forgiveness is a gift you give yourself.

Example: Ever heard someone apologize, but in a snide or sarcastic tone? You knew that it wasn't an apology it was just a ploy to end the conversation. Apologize only when you sincerely mean it. If you do not in the moment, then take a break. Go back and do so once you genuinely feel that you're ready to.

These are general principles that are meant to shape how we think about our own behaviours and attitudes in our relationships in general. Focus in on one or two that resound with you and work towards adopting them in your life. Once you do, then you can choose a couple more. One method for doing so would be to write the key concept down and put it somewhere you can see it every single day. Look at the words, notice how they feel, and reflect on them regularly. Begin to notice what changes are showing up in your relationships. *Insha'Allah* you will notice more compassion and empathy emerging.

Behaviours that damage relationships

Ask yourself this question, "How am I contributing to the issues in my most challenging relationship?" This is, of course, an extremely difficult question to ask. It makes the assumption that there is something that you are doing to contribute to the problem. Neither you, nor anyone else would like to think that they are doing something to hurt their loved ones. However, we are all human, and though we may not intend to, we may sometimes do things inadvertently that can cause long-term damage to an important relationship. Take a moment to reflect on three behaviours that you may have had that might have contributed to an issue in the relationship:

1______________________________
2______________________________
3______________________________

How do you know that these behaviours were an issue? Did the other person tell you? What did you do after you had an understanding that this was an issue? Did you do something differently? How did the awareness shift your behaviour?

Each person will have his or her list of pet peeves. These are behaviours such as calling too much/ not enough, being untidy, not keeping to time and so on. However, there are some general behaviours that can, and will, be corrosive to any relationship. These are not about doing specific things, but instead about behaviours that come from our general attitude towards the relationship, how we approach conflict, and how we communicate. These behaviours can be thought of as general pitfalls to forming good relationships with any other person, whether it be your spouse, child, a colleague or a community member. These behaviours are best avoided. Take a look at what they are and allow yourself time to think about whether any of these apply to you. If you find that you can relate to some of them, then ask yourself to explore how you carry out these behaviours in your own specific way. I have written them in a personal "you" form, not to imply that you might be doing this, it is, instead, to allow you to understand it in a more intimate way. Once you go through the list, do your own stock take of any that may apply.

Now let's take a look at what they are:

1. Putting the other person down

Putting another person down is saying something negative about any aspect of who they are as an individual. This is sometimes done to deliberately hurt, or sometimes it becomes habit. Remember that anger or hurt doesn't justify hurting the other person back. Once your anger fades you will regret what you said, but the damage to the relationship may be permanent. This behaviour can be deeply damaging to the other person's sense of self, and will, most likely, damage the relationship quite severely.

Example: You call your child "stupid" or "idiot" when he or she spills something, or gets a low mark. This can be damaging to them in the long term.

2. Holding resentments

Holding resentments means that you hold on to the negative memory of what someone did to you, even if the other person has apologized. Holding a grudge might feel like you are punishing the other person, and it might be so but it also destroys any possibility for the relationship to be repaired. You also tend to relive the negative emotions each time you remember the events, which magnifies them further with each recall. Holding resentments hurts you and damages the relationship further.

Example: Your spouse didn't take your side with his/her parents. You still remember it, even though it took place a decade ago, and the issue still comes up when you argue. Can you sense the lack of trust that still remains?

3. Playing the "blame" game

Playing the blame game can be tied to the above behaviour quite closely. Blaming the other person means that you hold him or her responsible for all that happened; they were at fault and you were the victim. Blame creates a negative spiral, because if one person feels blamed, he or she will retaliate with the same. This will lead to a deadlock in the relationship. If you allow yourself to take a breath, and observe from a more distant perspective, you might notice that you had a part to play as well. Letting the blame go will allow you to see the bigger picture, and perhaps change the way you relate to the other person.

Example: You hear your son or daughter complain about the maths teacher because they are getting a poor mark. It becomes a story through the whole academic year: the more they hate their teacher, the worse their grades seem to get.

4. Retaliation

To retaliate means to return harsh words or actions in reply to the other person's words or actions. This "eye for an eye" approach kills relationships. Each time we retaliate with words or actions, we escalate a bad situation into something worse. The next time you feel tempted to retaliate, take a deep breath and remove yourself from the situation.

Example: Someone sends a nasty email to an ex, and the ex responds with an equally nasty email. Soon there is an exchange of more than ten emails that have escalated to name-calling, and perhaps even bullying or threats. In a situation like this, no one ever really has the last word.

5. Sarcasm

This is one of the most common ways through which many people damage relationships. Sarcasm is speaking in a tone that makes the other person feel insulted or mocked. It may not be so much about the words, but sarcasm definitely shows through in your tone. Avoid this, as insulting another is definitely not conducive to a healthy relationship.

Example: Sarcasm is commonly seen within certain group dynamics. If you find that one person in the group is the one that everyone is "lovingly" making fun of, they are more often than not using sarcastic tones to do so. Ask the person at the receiving end of the "humour" how they really feel about it and they will admit to feeling ridiculed.

6. "Constructive" criticism

People often give "constructive criticism" with the best intentions in mind. This is one of those phrases that is so commonly used, that we often don't think about what the words truly mean. Let's break the expression down and see. Constructive means that it relates to building something or someone up. However, criticism is all about breaking something or someone down. If we put these two together, then one nullifies the other doesn't it? They simply can't go together. People often give constructive criticism by mentioning everything that the other person is doing wrong. There's hardly any mention of what's being done well. This leaves the receiver disempowered and perhaps confused as well. Instead of giving someone constructive criticism, give them feedback instead. We will discuss feedback in more detail later in the book, and talk about a wonderful exercise that teaches how to give feedback.

Example: Your child is taking a writing course during the summer. You go and meet with the teacher to get some feedback. All that the teacher mentions, is that your child is "slower than" the other kids and is unclear in her communication. She makes no mention of the fact that your child finished every single assignment on time.

7. Being vague about your expectations

It is human to have expectations. After all, forging a bond with someone will have some purpose behind it. If you are being vague about what you expect from the other person, there's no chance that this person can ever truly meet your expectations because they don't know what they are. The other person might do things that then disappoint you, and so a negative pattern will start to form in the relationship. Granted, you might not be doing this intentionally, but being vague means that you are not communicating your expectations clearly to the other person. Take some time to figure out what your expectations really are. If you feel that you are unclear yourself, begin by asking the other person what they think you expect from them – that will get the conversation rolling.

8. Mind reading

This is a tricky behaviour because many people might think that it shows how well they know the other person. Has anyone ever told you that they can read your mind? How did that feel? At times, it might feel like a wonderfully connected moment, and at other times it can cause people to grow apart. Mind reading essentially means that you allow your assumptions to lead you and become the "truth". This behaviour is dangerous because it might be that you are listening to your assumptions and not to the other person. This behaviour can cause the other person to become frustrated because they don't feel heard or acknowledged. If you perhaps fall into this behaviour without realizing, then aim to build the habit of checking in to see if you are on the right track.

Example: Two friends are making plans to go out to the movies. One of them decides which movie they will see because she assumes that both of them like horror movies. She only found out that her friend hates them because she walked out during the show!

What you resist, persists!

The list of behaviours that we just talked about is aimed to raise awareness towards some of the things that we might be doing, unintentionally, that can really ruin our relationships. If you look closer, you might notice that they are all behaviours that one might *impose on* another person whereas the best relationships are built in harmony *with* someone else. These behaviours also stem from certain attitudes, or even certain fears. For example, we might be afraid to say what we truly expect, and that's why we can't voice our needs. The aim here is to raise awareness so that we might begin to notice where we need to make changes. Having said that, you may feel that you don't need to make any changes. Perhaps you've done everything right, but the relationship (the one you identified earlier in the chapter) still isn't working. The entire conversation that we have been having through this chapter is not about assigning blame at all; instead, it is about raising awareness.

Okay so let's assume for a moment that you have been doing everything the correct way. You don't see yourself doing anything corrosive; instead, you have been adopting the principles already. So what's the reason why things aren't working? Is it that the other person is just beyond help, or might it be that there may still be something that you could do differently?

Shifting a relationship is one of the most challenging tasks a human being can take on because it requires a very candid look at one's own attitudes and behaviours. So I invite you keep an open mind here. Remember that whatever we resist tends to stay the same. This is because my own resistance will create a loop. For example, if I resist the fact that I am critical of my child or spouse, then I will continue speaking to him or her in a critical way and the other's person's reaction will be negative. The longer I continue to be critical, the longer the pattern will continue and the relationship will continue to deteriorate. Unless I become aware of my own critical behaviour, the loop will most likely continue as its been set up. Awareness is the key to any lasting change! Once we have awareness, we cannot ignore what's happening, and that is the biggest motivation to make lasting changes. I invite you to go back through this chapter and explore it further. Think about one or two things that may be minor, but if they were changed, might make a significant difference to that one relationship you want to improve. The most wonderful result of all will be that it will shift how you relate to yourself!

Let's summarise the main points:

- We defined what a "relationship" is.
- We explored your own motivation to change a relationship that might not be working.
- We looked at some general principles that apply to all relationships.
- We talked about some behaviours to avoid because they can be corrosive.

2.
Communication: The Work of Relationships

And fulfil the covenant of Allah when you have made a covenant, and do not break the oaths after making them fast, and you have indeed made Allah a surety for you; surely Allah knows what you do.

Qur'an 16:91

Verily, Allah will say on the Day of Resurrection: Where are those who love each other for the sake of My glory? Today, I will shelter them in My shade on a day when there is no shade but Mine.

Prophet Muhammad (pbuh)

I hope that the first chapter left you thinking about relationships slightly differently. Maintaining relationships is a choice, so when we choose to be in a relationship with someone, we need to also choose to do the work it takes to maintain that bond – whether we realize this or not.

The work of relationships is the "relating" or "connecting" to the other person. Relating or connecting can also be thought of as communicating; all these words can be used to describe the same thing. But what are they really describing? Ask yourself the following question and make a note of your answer.

What is communication?

Communication is generally thought of as one person transmitting information to another. One person sends it, and the other receives it as intended. This is a valid form of communication, especially when we are communicating "to" someone by giving him or her some news for example. However, communicating "to" people doesn't really work in every situation because we also receive communications.

All this exchange of information can become complicated, and that's why we experience variances in our relationships. Some of our relationships flow well, whereas others may feel like a total train wreck. We might be communicating the same way we always do yet this one person seems to always take things the wrong way. Every conversation becomes a conflict. Sound familiar? Communication isn't always as simple as saying something, and it be understood in the way we want. What makes communication complicated is that it is a two-way street. This is why our communication may be very effective with one person, yet completely ineffective with another. Once we are aware of what effective communication might look like, we can strive towards achieving that quality that in various relationships. So let's go ahead and define it:

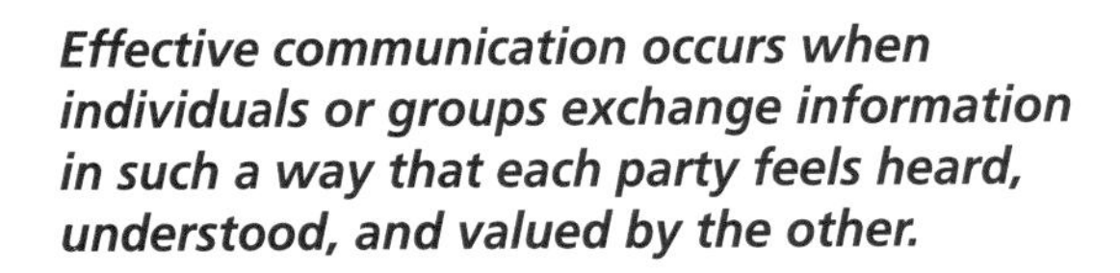

What's the main thing that jumped out for you from this definition? The real key is that communication is effective when *both* parties feel heard and understood. Recall a certain friendship or relationship that was difficult for you. How did you communicate with that person? Do you feel that you tried your best to understand this person? Did they do the same for you?

The W.I.F.M. attitude can get in the way

Generally, human beings like to be acknowledged and understood. In fact, this is how we experience belonging and connection in the world. Even though we may have the best of intentions, at times our communication might become a little more self-centred than we might want to admit. This might well happen without our conscious awareness.

Let's think about a general example to understand this better. Imagine that you are at a networking event; it can be social or for work. You are mingling with people and enjoying yourself. Soon, you join a group of 3–4 people who are busy chatting. You notice that two of them are very relaxed, their body language is open and they are enjoying getting to know each other. One of them asks a question, and the other responds and vice versa. The third person who is there keeps interrupting them. He isn't really listening; instead, he keeps interrupting and putting his opinions across. As you observe, you notice that this person has a different energy; it almost seems that he is in that group to serve his own agenda. After a few minutes of this, the two people who were enjoying the chat excuse themselves, and continue talking over to the side.

What do you think happened here? That one person who joined the group wasn't really thinking about the other people he was talking with. He was thinking about what he wanted to get out of the conversation. He was running an internal program that we can refer to as W.I.F.M. or "What's In It For Me?".

If we approach any communication by focusing on only the outcome that we want, the chances are that the communication will be ineffective. We might not be doing it consciously, but we might still be really attached to getting something from the other person. This behaviour is very transparent with children, when they keep asking for something. However, with adult communication it might be hidden, or unconscious.

How do you know that W.I.F.M. has taken over?

The biggest sign that our communication is ineffective is that we will have broken rapport with the other person. We will be able to sense a distance, a disconnect and it will almost be like at one minute you felt connected, and the next moment it was gone. That is when you know that you've broken rapport.

What is rapport?

Rapport is a sign that effective communication is taking place. Let's take an example to understand this better. Think of one of your most healthy relationships for a moment. Close your eyes, and visualize this person. Notice their expression, how they look, and any other details. Now, take a moment to notice some of the thoughts that are coming up for you. Are you smiling? Are there good memories coming to mind? Now bring your attention to the last time you met him or her. How was the communication? Were you both sharing? Did you feel connected? Were you both listening to one another? That practice of building a connection in this way is known as rapport. Let's define it:

Rapport is the process of building a connection. Rapport also refers to the flow that can be seen, heard, and experienced when people are connecting with each other.

Building rapport requires that we use certain skills. Skills that help us build rapport include listening, noticing the other person's body language and so on. When we can allow ourselves to really observe and enjoy the other person for who they are, we can build rapport with them quite easily.

We will be exploring how to build rapport in exercises throughout this book, but for now, let's sum up the ideas so far, so that we can absorb them. A relationship begins when we intend to connect with someone. Choosing to create a relationship is the first step. The second step begins when we start communicating, sharing and connecting. This process of connecting is called building rapport. As we start being curious, trying to understand and acknowledge the other person, our rapport begins to deepen. We can then begin to sense our connection and enjoy the flow of the relationship. This sense of connection is also part of rapport. So rapport essentially is starting and maintaining effective communication with someone (and reaping the benefits).

So whenever you want to observe how a relationship is doing, notice the peoples' body language, their facial expressions, even some of their words. If you observe carefully, you will notice whether a connection is present or not. The signs of rapport indicate whether they are in a healthy bond or not. In fact, you can do the same thing for yourself. The next time you're having a great chat with a close friend, just observe for yourself. Notice how your body language is, how the other person's is, what your facial expressions are and so on. Just keep this learning quiet, and to yourself. With practice, you will be able to see with whom, and where you are able to build rapport, and when you feel challenged to do so. With practice, you will be able to notice the moment that rapport has broken, so you can begin your efforts to re-establish it then and there. You can begin the work of repairing the relationship in that moment.

Each one of us has our own unique way of communicating

As we will observe people, we might notice that everyone has a different way of expressing affection. For example, some people will give their time and may appreciate being given time. Another person may like to give and receive gifts. Think back to a time when you did something that you thought was very loving, however the other person didn't appreciate it in quite the same way. This is not because the other person doesn't care (it may have felt like that); instead, it may be because he or she experiences being loved in a different way. This is why it is very important to understand communication, and appreciate how people communicate in their own unique ways. Let's begin this process with a little exercise. The exercise below will raise your awareness on how you prefer to communicate.

Exercise 2.1: Understanding How You Connect

Method: Answer the multiple-choice questions with the first answer that comes to mind

1. **At the end of a long day, what I would appreciate most would be:**
   a. Someone making me a nice cup of tea.
   b. A chat about my day, asking how it went.
   c. A warm hug to relax and unwind.
   d. A few words of encouragement.
   e. A nice meal as a surprise.

2. **I have been working so hard at my job and my work has led to some good outcomes. I would feel most appreciated by my boss if he/ she were to:**
   a. Give me a raise/promotion for my hard work.
   b. Say a few words of encouragement.
   c. Come and spend some time, find out how things are going.
   d. Congratulations and a handshake would do.
   e. Find out what I really need to go to the next level – and help me get there.

3. I go out of my way for my friends. I know they really care about me, but what would allow me to feel that they are really there for me is:
   a. Sending a card on my birthday.
   b. Make time to meet – at least once a month, or whenever possible.
   c. Encourage me when I'm feeling down.
   d. Helping me out with babysitting once in a while – like I do things for them.
   e. Just come over and give me a hug when I need cheering up.

4. When I want to show someone that I really care, the thing that I am most likely to do is:
   a. Send them a card or flowers to surprise them.
   b. Make time and plan a weekend trip together, or spend the day catching up.
   c. Give them a huge hug, or whatever is appropriate!
   d. Offer to help them run errands or get something done.
   e. Tell them "I love you", "I care about you", "I miss you", etc.

5. I show my family that I care by:
   a. Cooking their favourite meal for them.
   b. Paying all the bills, providing for them.
   c. Spending quality time at the weekends.
   d. Giving them all hugs, playing with the kids.
   e. Encouraging them to pursue their own dreams and goals – always offering positive words.

Step 2: Understanding your answers

There are five main categories of how we express affection. Let's look at what they are:

1. Helping actions.
2. Spending quality time with loved ones.
3. Showing your affection through words (expressing/ receiving validation).
4. Showing love through physical touch.
5. Giving and receiving gifts.

Observations:

Now take a look at your answers. What patterns do you notice?
Which categories do you fit in to?
Do you prefer to do the same things for others that you would like for yourself?
How effective are they?
How similar or different do you now think your loved one's preferences lie in how they feel cared for?

We normally have one or two preferred ways of showing affection. Customarily, the way that we give affection is normally the same way in which we prefer to receive it. Think of a time when you felt really pampered and loved. What did the other person do or say that germinated those feelings? Memories of that nature will also support you in clarifying your own preferred expression of affection.

Our communications need to be adapted

Each person will have a unique way of giving and receiving affection. You might prefer someone to spend quality time with you, but they may prefer you to encourage them with positive words. It is dangerous to assume that the people in our life will appreciate everything we do, or express affection the same way we like to. In fact, the way they prefer to receive affection may be very different to our own. They will not be able to appreciate our gestures the way they are meant, especially if their own mode of receiving is totally different.

The work of relationships entails expressing affection and love in a way that the other person actually experiences that affection. If we do not communicate our care in a way that the other person understands, the effort will actually be wasted because it won't achieve the desired outcome. All of the methods that we talked about in the previous exercise are all modes of communication. For our communication to genuinely get through, it has to land in a way that the other person experiences it as it was intended. So if we are expressing love, we would need to express it in the way that the other person experiences it as love. I imagine communication sounds more complicated now. So how do we really make sure that our messages of affection are effective? How do we ensure that all parties can create and connect with the common purpose? In order for our communication to be more effective, we need to understand *how* to communicate effectively. We will be exploring various techniques throughout this book, but, for now, we need to create a solid foundation from which to work.

General principles of communication

The best way to improve our communication skills is to understand the basics first. To start with, let's confirm that all our actions are communications of some kind. Sounds pretty simple, so why does communication become so complicated and difficult? The reason why communication is difficult with some people and not others is because each human being comes from a totally unique perspective. A certain behaviour may be fine with one and completely offend another. This is why a general foundation is so important. We are all human, so there must be some commonality among us all. Given that there may be a way to connect through our similarities, wouldn't it be useful to have some general principles that govern all communication?

Indeed, there are some general principles regarding communication, that come from neuro-linguistic programming. This is a field of applied psychology that's often used in coaching. Let's think of these principles as our foundation, from which we can build further. Once we understand, accept, and apply these principles, we can then make adjustments for specific situations (and people). Creating a conscious process will help us be truly effective in improving our relationships. So let's take a look at these general principles and aim to understand them.

1. We are never not communicating!

In other words, we are *always* communicating! We are transmitting messages even when we aren't saying anything, or are by ourselves. Remember the last time you tried to silence that voice in your head that was going a million miles a minute. What was that like? Were you successful? This voice says really discouraging things at times, doesn't it? What would it be like if you could catch it doing that, and steer it in another direction right then and there, wouldn't that be helpful? Being aware that we are always communicating helps us become aware of the quality of the message that we are transmitting, to others and ourselves. We might think that we aren't saying anything when we are being silent, but that couldn't be further from the truth.

2. The response we receive tells us what our communication means

Recall a time when you had an argument with a loved one, and you didn't even realize that you had upset them. This is a very common problem and it occurs mainly because we are unaware of how our words and actions are actually impacting the other person. This principle makes us aware of one very important aspect of any relationship: the other person's response to what we said or did is how they actually interpreted our communication. What we truly meant to say isn't the important thing here – *what's important is how the other person understood it.*

Start noticing how other people respond to what you say and do, and this will give you feedback on how well your desired message is getting across. If the other person is reacting in anger or hurt, then that means you need to adjust how you are sending your message. If you keep doing or saying the same things, you will keep getting the same result and this will cause a vicious cycle which might be tough to break later on. Awareness here will make a huge difference. Once you notice the pattern, change your approach a little and do something different.

3. We can choose to respond to communications

Consider a relationship that's struggling right now. How did you reply any time this person said something that you found hurtful? Did you react immediately, or did you take a few minutes (or more) to respond?

The difference between a reaction and a response is that a reaction is often instant and emotional, whereas a response is thought out and more measured. A person could either respond or react: the choice is theirs. So, the next time someone says something that doesn't feel good, take a deep breath and allow your emotions to settle first before responding. By choosing to take your time to respond, you will give yourself the opportunity to calm down and then say what you really want to. Reactions can often escalate difficult situations so this is something important to keep in mind.

4. Communication occurs with our whole being not just our words

Remember the exercise earlier in the chapter? It pointed to the idea that communication involves our thoughts, body language, actions, and words. In fact, our non-verbal communication signals send very subtle messages about how we are feeling. Think of a time when someone you love wasn't saying anything to you, but you knew that they were hurt or upset by some communication from you. How did you know? Was it their silence? Maybe their body language was closed, or perhaps they didn't greet you or call and check in like they do every day. Many of us think that our words are the main form of how we communicate, but this is not the whole truth. Become aware of your body language, thoughts, and actions with people you aren't getting along with right now. You might notice that you are sending out a less than positive message yourself.

5. If you don't believe in what you're communicating, it will show through

Ever been in a situation where someone is saying something but you get the vibe that they really mean something else? Whenever we have self-doubt, or we say things that we don't truly believe, our bodies will give us away. Our thoughts and beliefs have a way of coming through in our body language. It is essential to remember this. So the next time you are having an important conversation, check in with yourself first to see if you truly believe what you are saying. If you do not, you will come across as insincere. It is better to say "I don't know" or "let me get back to you" rather than say or promise things that you might not be sure of, or believe in. So create a practice of checking in with yourself. Are you saying what you truly believe to be true? Are you making a promise that you really feel that you can deliver on? If you do, then go ahead, if not, then it might be a good time to recommit to something else. Remember this is just as valid with the promises you make to yourself as it is with others.

6. Each and every human being has a unique model of the world

This principle is one of the most essential ones of all. In fact, if we can remember this one, then we can apply the others a lot more easily. Let's look at this in another way. Take a moment to observe your fingerprints. Know that there is only *one* set of fingerprints just like yours – your own. *SubhanAllah*, every single human being has a unique set of fingerprints. That is why they are used for identification purposes.

Similar to your fingerprints, the exact way you think is unlike any other person on earth. The combination of your upbringing, culture, beliefs, and the way you interpret your experiences make only one of you. We all share certain things in common with others, but our way of thinking is just as unique as our fingerprints and our DNA. This is so important to understand because when we communicate with others, we often make the assumption that the other person will understand what we mean. But if we realize that the way that they look at the world is unique, we realize that we need to explain what we mean, and to understand what they mean, rather than to take that understanding for granted.

There are many things that connect us. We all have similar needs for food, shelter, rest, social connection, etc. These commonalities help us to empathize with others and share our human experiences. However, when it comes to relationships, it is important to keep in mind that even though we share experiences with our families, loved ones and communities, other members of the group may still view that shared experience in their own unique way, or experience it differently to us. Of course, any two people may see a lot of things in the same way, but it's nothing to be alarmed about if there are differences. For example, two people can read a book and glean completely different things from it. So the next time you are having an important conversation, keep in mind that the other person may well have a different perspective to yours. Give him or her room to express their views on the topic and you will be able to create rapport more easily.

7. The mind and body are one system

We commonly tell ourselves that "it's mind over matter" and we can achieve something if we "put our minds to it". We do this because we have heard this a lot, and so we take it to be true. These common expressions are, however, quite misleading. If you think about it, these expressions imply that the mind is in control and overrides our bodies. On the contrary, our minds work in tandem with our bodies and guide them all the time. What happens in the mind, happens in the body. The mind's primary purpose is to keep us alive and well; it does what it does to fulfil this purpose. For example, if you are having stressful thoughts, your body will feel the symptoms through a fast heartbeat, sweaty palms, or an anxious feeling within your chest. These symptoms explain that our minds and bodies work as one system. Our bodies are also communicating with us, as are our minds. In fact, it's difficult to assess which comes first; because we are essentially experiencing life through the body, but it is the mind that interprets the experience.

When we start becoming aware of what our bodies are conveying, we can often understand the deeper thoughts and beliefs that come up in order to interpret those symptoms. Our bodies can be a gateway to understanding ourselves better. Remember, when you are noticing something in another person's body language, go with the cues their body language is giving off, even if their words are saying something else. Keep in mind that you will be interpreting what you notice, so you may want to ask them if what you sense is correct or not.

8. If you are stressed, your ability to communicate effectively will be compromised

Stress is an indication that we are in a state of fight–flight–freeze, which definitely impacts how we communicate. Communication requires that we are able to observe and listen to the other person without becoming judgemental or defensive. Stress takes us into a state of fight – flight – freeze and this is a state where everything is seen as a threat. In this state, we cannot communicate effectively. By catching ourselves when we are stressed, we can start implementing some strategies to relax and come back to the conversation at a better time.

Observe the learnings

What do you notice as you learn about these principles? Upon reflection, you will notice that these actually refer to how human beings generally function in life and in relationships. Start applying them, perhaps one or two at a time, and you will begin to raise your awareness on what is working and what needs to change in how you communicate.

As we understand ourselves and try to create more fulfilling relationships, we will be able to enhance our rapport with others. Rapport, again, is that process of building and maintaining a relationship. You can see, feel and experience the rapport you have with another person. So as you practice communicating in difference ways, you will learn new ways of thinking and behaving that will support you in enhancing rapport with others.

How does rapport connect with empathy?

Empathy with another person can take our relationships to a more meaningful level. Empathy essentially means that a person can experience what another person is experiencing, by walking in the other person's shoes. To have empathy means that we can understand, even adopt how the other person thinks and feels, and what they experience. People often mistake empathy and rapport to be the same thing, but they are not.

To create rapport with someone means that we start building a relationship and this process happens by using a set of skills. We often create rapport with people using many of these skills innately, however, we can also learn certain skills that will support us in building rapport. Rapport begins with the acceptance that the other person will have his or her own unique view of the world. By having this belief in place, we start with a certain acceptance of the other person; this acceptance gives us the opportunity to build empathy. In essence then, building rapport is the gateway to then building empathy with another human being. We will talk about rapport building in later chapters as well, as it is an ongoing process.

Let's summarise the main points:

Relationships require some work. We learned that communication is the "work" of relationships. We also learned that communication occurs with our whole being. Given that communication with others can sometimes be challenging, we explored certain principles that can apply to all communication.

- We defined what effective communication is.
- We explored the various ways in which we communicate.
- We talked about principles that relate to all communication.
- We discussed that rapport is the process of building a relationship, and that you see, hear and experience its presence.

3. Building a Compassionate Relationship with Yourself

And the soul and Him Who made it perfect, Then He inspired it to understand what is right and wrong for it; He will indeed be successful who purifies it, And he will indeed fail who corrupts it.

Qur'an 91:7–10

Whoever seeks forgiveness in abundance, Allah will give him relief from every distress and an outlet from every source of anxiety.

Prophet Muhammad (pbuh)

Imagine that you are at a large community event. There are speeches and workshops taking place, and you are there to present. You are sitting in the hallway preparing for your workshop that's about to take place in the next hour. As you are preparing, a friend of yours walks by absolutely distraught. You stop her and enquire about what happened. She tells you that her talk didn't go well, that she thought that she made huge mistakes, the crowd didn't like her and she won't be invited to speak again. You listen patiently to what she's saying, and then you offer her some consolation. You advise her, encourage her and give her positive feedback until she's feeling better.

Now take a moment to focus on your own life. Are you this compassionate with yourself when things go wrong? How do you speak to yourself during such times? Are you kind, or harsh? Often, we are compassionate with others, yet very harsh with ourselves. Compassion encourages us to do better, to try again. Harsh criticism can stop us from overcoming the challenge because we feel unable to. So in this chapter, we will explore what compassion is, and how to develop a more compassionate relationship with ourselves.

How do you speak to yourself?

The most lasting relationship we can ever have is the one with ourselves, obviously, because we can only ever be in our own skin. Having said that, many of us speak to ourselves far more unkindly then we ever would to anyone else. Have you ever thought about the quality of your internal conversations? If we raise our awareness on the subject, we will realize that our self-talk has a direct impact on how we feel about ourselves, others, and life in general. There will be another exercise on this subject a bit later on, but for now, just take a moment to answer the multiple-choice questions below.

Exploration: My relationship with myself

1. **Each time I do something well, I**
   a. Take a moment to acknowledge myself, at least verbally.
   b. I ask myself, "Now what's next."
   c. What's the big deal, I didn't do anything important.
   d. I hope that the person I did it for might notice.

2. **Each time I make a mistake, I**
   a. Make sure to write it down (so I don't repeat it).
   b. I know I should have known better.
   c. Forgive myself and get back on track.
   d. Tell my friends/ family about it, and discuss.

3. **I think that my self-confidence to do things is**
   a. Very Low.
   b. Low.
   c. OK, average, I guess.
   d. I'm confident on the outside, but I'm often scared on the inside.
   e. I'm confident in getting things done.

4. **When starting something new, I tell myself that**
   a. "It is going to be tough, and I know I will struggle."
   b. "I know I can't really do it, but I will try."
   c. "Give it your best shot, and see what happens."
   d. "You can do whatever you put your mind to."

5. **Each time I think about my accomplishments in life, I feel**
   a. Grateful that I've been able to achieve what I wanted.
   b. Don't really have any accomplishments.
   c. Angry because I know that I haven't achieved much.
   d. Jealous of my friends who've achieved their dreams.

What did you notice from this exercise? Go back and observe your answers, what do you notice about how you speak to yourself. Are you mostly kind, or are you now realizing that you are quite harsh with yourself?

The quality of our inner relationship will impact all others

This book is about supporting you to cultivate stronger relationships in various areas of your life. But what if your own view of yourself is harsh, how would that impact your view of other people? Is it possible to think that everyone else is doing better than you, and never feel resentful? It's not realistic to think that we can be good to others, while being harsh with ourselves. Bring to mind someone who you experience as harsh. Are they strict? Their words harsh? observe them for some time, if possible. Notice what they say about themselves, or their work in conversation. You will start to see a pattern. People who are harsh with others are generally very hard on themselves. The point here is that if we want to have more compassionate and kind relationships with others, we might need to cultivate that a little bit for ourselves first. Think of compassion as a learned behaviour, you practise it on yourself first, and then have it there to practise with others.

The starting point is to have a solid relationship with yourself because if you don't have anything to give yourself, you really can't give anything to others. Have you ever been on an airplane? Remember the safety video that's played? Every airline I've ever been on advises the same thing; put on your own oxygen mask before helping others (even your own children). This is because they recognize that you have to be OK in order to be of use to others. Take a note of your answers to the following question:

What would a compassionate relationship with myself make possible in my life and relationships?

Some possible answers might be:

- I would be more empowered to do things.
- I would have a better opinion of myself.

- I would feel "good enough, strong enough, pretty enough, etc."
- I would like what I see in the mirror.

The first step to building more self-compassion is to first notice how much self-compassion you currently practise. One effective method is to notice one's language. Our language occurs in a pattern; there's a stimulus and then a response. We see, hear, or experience something, and then we respond to it. For example, you see yourself in the mirror, and you have a thought, "I look tired" or "I look terrible today". Our self-talk is how we communicate internally. The tone and word choice we use indicates how we feel about ourselves.

The first exercise you did gave you some insight on how you're currently thinking and responding to situations. I invite you to take this awareness a little bit deeper now. The following exercise is designed to raise your awareness towards your tone and language towards yourself, and then towards others and life as well.

Exercise 3.1: What Am I Really Saying?

Outcome: To raise your awareness on how you really treat yourself, especially when you are on your own.

Method: Get a notebook or a journal that you like to write in. Keep it on your nightstand before you go to bed. Arrange to wake up about fifteen minutes earlier than your scheduled time. As you wake up, sit up in bed and pay attention to the voice in your head. Write down everything that comes to mind. Then close the book.

At night: Just before going to sleep: take a few minutes to just write whatever the inner voice is saying; in other words, whatever is coming to mind. Close the book and go to sleep.

Repeat this process for a minimum of three days, and a maximum for seven days. This amount of time should give you a good idea of the theme and tone of your self-talk.

Observation: Once the time you committed to doing this is over, take some time to read what you wrote. Then note down:

What's the first thing that came to mind as you read what you had written?
What are you noticing about the tone of your voice?
How does it feel when you speak to yourself in this manner?

On a scale from 1–10, 10 being the highest, how compassionate is your tone of voice?

1 2 3 4 5 6 7 8 9 10

Is the tone:

- Like a parent?
- Like a good friend?
- Like a judge?
- Like you normally are? What tone would that be?

What else is coming to mind?

Why am I being harsh?

Did the exercises in the previous section surprise you? Were you saddened to discover how you talk to yourself? Human behaviour usually has two main components. The first component is that it is learned, and the second is, that it serves a deeper purpose. Even negative behaviours have a deeper, positive purpose to them but we just don't often know what they are on a conscious level. We develop behaviours to meet a need. The behaviour may be negative, but the need is often a positive, human need. The really good news here is that we can replace the negative behaviour with a productive one, once we know what need we are trying to meet. That's if, we are ready and willing to.

For example, there was a lady who asked me to coach her mother some years ago. She was extremely worried that her mother's health was deteriorating and she was refusing to give up her chain smoking. Upon the lady's insistence, I went to talk to her mother. After spending some time with her, and exploring with her, she openly said that smoking gave her happiness. She was clear that there was nothing anyone could say or do to convince her to stop. The deeper value was so fundamentally important to her that she was unwilling to give it up. Her daughter was extremely upset and frustrated, but she was helpless in this situation because her mother was unwilling to be coached around this and that was her personal choice. However, many other clients I've worked with have noticed that their negative behaviours are meeting a need – and they have found positive alternatives to meet the same need. This is possible provided a person is dedicated to making this shift and willing to be coachable.

As Muslims, one of the most important goals we aspire to is to fulfil our potential. This also means that we avoid behaviours that will harm us, or other people. So take comfort in the idea that even though you might be harsh with yourself, rest assured that there is a positive need and a higher purpose underneath. It may seem like there isn't but it's still worth taking a look. I invite you to ponder the following question (use the version you prefer), and write down whatever comes to mind:

What is being harsh with myself giving me?
or
What is my self-talk giving me?

You may have heard yourself think "nothing" or maybe a negative sentiment of some kind. Finding a closed answer is quite normal at first. Persevere with it, and ask this question a few times, and keep documenting your answers. You will get to a certain point where you will feel that you have reached something deeper. Look out for "value" words such as "motivation, protection, the push, encouragement" and so on. This is challenging to take on by yourself, but imagine that I am sitting in front of you, coaching you through this process. Allow yourself to let go and really explore.

Shifting behaviour becomes far easier once we know what's at stake if we don't.

Imagine that someone realizes that being harsh with himself is his own inner way of motivating himself to deal with life. However, each time he is harsh with himself, he feels pulled down as well. The intention is positive, but the result is negative. He ends up criticizing himself each time he tells himself that he "just isn't getting it right, he must push harder, or do better" which may pull him down more than motivate him. This creates a vicious cycle that becomes hard to break. One side says to do more, and the other is disempowered to take action; this only leads to more frustration and lower self-esteem in the long run.

The part of us that talks to us in these disempowering ways is aiming to encourage, but the result is the opposite. We are discussing this as a general pattern that occurs. Take a moment to notice if you are doing something similar. If you are, then notice how you feel with this self-talk. Are you getting more positive results? I guess possibly not.

If we are to break this cycle, then we must become aware of the real intention behind this negative self-talk. Figure that out, and you can then choose a more productive channel to achieve the same results. Look at the table below as an example:

Table 3.1: Exploring your current self-talk

Current self-talk	How I feel when I say/ hear these things	Possible intention of the self-talk. What does it want for me?	Possible new behaviour
I can't believe I said/did that. I shouldn't have.	I feel bad, guilty, at fault. I should have done better.	Wants me to improve. Handle situations effectively.	Plan important conversations. Take deep breaths before reacting.
I'm so stupid. How could I be so stupid?	I feel dumb, stupid and incapable. I feel shouted at.	Wants me to think, to be sharp. Smart maybe.	Forgive myself for making a mistake. Get back on track.
I'm so ugly. I'm fat. Can't even lose weight, what's wrong with me?	I feel ugly and unlovable. I feel unattractive. It affects my self-esteem.	Wants to give me a kick to do something. Maybe wants me to diet properly.	Find a plan that I can stick with. Maybe do it slowly. Be kind to myself. Have a massage now and again.
I am not good at maths.	It blocks me. I somehow just can't think with the test in front of me. I go blank.	To study harder, to pass my exams.	Make study plans. Figure out what I tell myself instead, especially before an exam.

Did you see yourself in any of these examples? What is your own self-talk like? How well is it working for you? Are you able to motivate yourself through it? Are you being harsh with yourself, without even realizing? The interesting thing to note is that self-talk isn't an evil thing that is imposed on us. In fact, it is our own voice that becomes conditioned as we grow up. We often take on the tone and words of our primary carers, family and loved ones.

Explore the tone of your self-talk. Note who in your family has, or had, a similar way of speaking to themselves; this is to observe and compare, not to judge. Again, they will have also had the best of intentions, but the behaviour expressing the intentions (the self-talk) was not the most productive. The issue isn't with the intention instead it is with the behaviour that's trying to fulfil that intention. Once you become aware of the pattern, you can do something to change it. The main component required to create this change is to bring some compassion into how you speak to and treat yourself. We will call this self-compassion. Let's define what self-compassion is:

Self-compassion is when a person can talk to himself or herself with kindness, and is able to accept the reality of his or her behaviour, and the situation, as it is in the moment.

When you bring self-compassion into your conversations with yourself, it means that you can notice what you did wrong, and accept it. Instead of spending your energy telling yourself off, you can spend that same energy doing something to rectify it. Recall a scenario where you were very hard on yourself. How would it have been different if you could have been a little kinder to yourself? What might you have done differently?

Being self-compassionate means I'm letting myself off the hook

Do you still think that being harsh on yourself helps you? What if you could be firm with yourself, but in a loving way? The two can go together. If we are treating ourselves with some compassion, we can accept our mistakes without resisting them. What happened, happened. Now we can get on with doing what needs to be done in order to resolve any issues, or do better next time.

Being compassionate does not mean that we allow mediocre performance or excuse our mistakes. On the contrary, some compassion will save us a whole lot of energy. There won't be any vicious circle of criticism that's followed by resistance. Remember that self-shaming isn't causing any change. It demotivates instead. Practising self-compassion allows us to maintain a healthy sense of self-esteem instead.

Think of someone you know who has a really high sense of self-esteem. Ask this person how he or she deals with a mistake or an unexpected result. Such people say they try to learn from their mistakes, forgive themselves and move on. You might notice that such people bring some compassion into how they speak to, and about, themselves. Our relationship with ourselves is shaped by so many factors including our environment, upbringing, religious values, education and so on. This exercise on self-talk sheds light on how we view ourselves. However, this may be a difficult exercise for some. Perhaps you are someone who needs a context to understand how you currently think about yourself. The following exercise will help you get to the same result, but in a different way. Give it a go, especially if you found the writing one challenging.

Exercise 3.2: Exploring How You "See" Yourself

Outcome: This is another way to assess how you feel about yourself.

Method: It might be useful to have your phone, or an audio recorder for this. Stand in front of a full-length mirror. Begin to observe what you see, and notice the thoughts that come to mind. Vocalize those thoughts and allow them to be recorded. Do this for about five minutes, or for as long as is comfortable. Aim to make your observations as thorough as you can.

Observation: Listen to the recording the next day, or a few days later. Make a note of the following:

1. I noticed that the way I speak about myself is ______________________

____

2. The tone of my thoughts about myself is ______________________

____

3. The level of compassion that I have for myself is ______________________

____

1 2 3 4 5 6 7 8 9 10

Pretty harsh — Very Compassionate

4. What did I see, hear, and experience that tells me that I am at this number? ______________________

5. How I would really like to speak to myself, and think about myself? ______________________

6. I am now ready to be more compassionate with myself because it will allow me to ______________________

Self-esteem and compassion are connected

The main reason why people develop a harsh tone with themselves is because they start to judge their own value by external measures. The way most of us normally measure our own value is by how we look, how much money we have, where we live and so on. All of that should be fine in theory, but severe problems can occur when something on the outside changes. For example, if you lose your job, have an accident or disfigurement, grow older, put on weight, etc., then all the value that this thing gave you will also disappear. To build a stronger relationship with oneself, we would first need to explore what we use to value ourselves, and then perhaps think about self-esteem a little bit differently. I defined self-esteem in my first book, and we are going to use the same definition here.

The value you place on yourself, which enables you to love and cherish who you are and take care of yourself accordingly.

We normally do place value on ourselves, but in relationship to external factors. If we continue to measure our worth in how much money we make for example, we would be back to having a self-esteem that fluctuates. In order for us to have a more compassionate relationship with ourselves, let's now begin with the idea that every human being has value because Allah has created him or her. You are valuable because Allah created you as a human being. The reason why our self-esteem shifts according to circumstances is because it is attached to those circumstances, and not to the virtue of being a human being. What makes it even more fragile is the fact that we forget to talk to ourselves with any compassion at all.

Okay, so you now appreciate that having compassion is important if you are to maintain a healthy relationship with yourself. Now the problem is that you've not really witnessed much of this, and don't know how it's done. The wonderful thing about being human, *alhamdulillah*, is the fact that we can adapt and change. We can learn how to be different, and to do things differently. Let's explore an exercise that will help you build a more compassionate relationship with yourself.

Exercise 3.3: Bringing In A Compassionate Guardian Visualization

Outcome: To support you in building a more compassionate relationship with yourself.

Method: Read the exercise instructions before you begin. It might be handy to record these instructions and then listen to them as you're doing the exercise. Do it in a way that suits you best.

Think about a certain personal issue that you have been trying to overcome. An example of such an issue would be overcoming procrastination, having trouble studying or concentrating, having trouble losing weight, quitting smoking and so on.

Close your eyes and bring your attention to this challenge. Think about the times that you have tried to overcome it, and have not yet succeeded; allow yourself to visualize this situation and create a movie. See yourself dealing with the situation, notice where you are, and what you're doing and so on. Notice the struggle and how you're trying to overcome it.

Now, imagine getting help from someone who can be a compassionate guide for you. This can be an Islamic role model, someone from your family, a wise elder, or someone you think of as a role model. Imagine that this person is now with you as a wise and compassionate guide. Imagine that he or she is present, and is speaking to you. Notice:

What is he or she saying to you?

How is this wise elder guiding you?

How is this guide showing you compassion with his or her words?

Observation: Imagine that this guide represents a compassionate part of yourself that already lies within you, wanting to be expressed. Choose a few key words that really spoke to you, and write them down. If they are based in a second person format, change them into the first person (from "you" to "I") and notice which feels better. Put these words up where you can see them every day. They will serve as a reminder to speak to yourself with kindness, especially when dealing with a challenge. Remind yourself that this is your own inner voice.

How much do you accept yourself?

Islam guides us to be compassionate, and we are encouraged to hide the flaws of our fellow Muslims. This is primarily to avoid gossiping or deliberately shaming each other. In the same way, we can stop shaming and blaming ourselves by toning our critical voice down through compassion. As we discussed earlier, our self-talk is shaped through our upbringing. The tone is shaped through our upbringing and the mechanism is one that responds to all the stimuli that we face on a moment-by-moment basis.

None of us can change the past or be free from imperfections or mistakes. Self-acceptance is the avenue that can free us from all the internal suffering and struggle that we impose on ourselves. The suffering doesn't come from our circumstances as much as from how we judge ourselves because of them. Self-acceptance can free us from that behaviour.

Self-acceptance is the practice of gently observing your internal self-talk and letting it go so you can focus on living your life by your deeper values and goals.

Remember that this self-talk can be positive or negative; it is the mechanism of how we respond to situations. It is the way our mind makes sense of the world around us in order to keep us healthy and well. Another point to note is that our self-talk emerges from our own past experience. Our brain uses interpretations of past events to create our internal chatter about the future. We can either choose to give in to it, or just observe it and gently let it go. Though bringing compassion into the picture helps, for some it cannot do enough to diminish our internal struggles completely. It may quieten them down, but they can still be there, because that sense of being less than "good enough" is still there.

Practising self-acceptance is a way to release ourselves from feeling "not good enough" because it is all about genuinely accepting what actually "is". The more we practise this "self-acceptance" and letting go, the more our internal struggles will quieten down. We may have more freedom and energy to just get on with things. It would improve our own relationship with ourselves because we would feel more at peace with the way we are. Let's look at how to practise self-acceptance:

Exercise 3.4: Observing Your Internal Judgments

Objective: The object of the exercise is to support you in observing your internal judgements and letting them go.

Method: This is an exercise of observation. Your aim is to focus on your thoughts and feelings as an observation, without engaging with them or allowing yourself to become "hooked".

Choose a time of day when you can be alone. Sit in a comfortable chair. Close your eyes, take a few deep breaths. Allow your attention to focus inwards. Just take some time to notice the sensations coming up in your body. Is there any pain or tightness? Does your body feel stressed or relaxed? How are your shoulders feeling? Observe the sensations, and then just let them be. Just accept that they are there. You could tell yourself, "Okay, you're there." Literally thank the sensation for being present.

Observe what thoughts are coming in. Just observe them, and allow them to be there. Just notice the thought. You may acknowledge it by saying "Okay" or whatever feels comfortable. Remember, that you are just observing and accepting what is there. If you find yourself engaging with the thoughts, just breathe deep and remind yourself that you are in "coach" position and come out.

Practice this observation exercise starting with a couple of minutes per day. You can take it up to as much as 30 minutes, whatever feels comfortable. Work with this exercise for a few days before proceeding to the next step.

How is the practice of self-acceptance going?

Some people may feel that self-compassion, and self-acceptance are avenues to stop themselves or others from being accountable. That is the opposite of what these behaviours are designed to achieve. If a person practises self-acceptance, then he or she can stop resisting all the internal criticism and just "sit" with how things are. This actually frees one up to notice opportunities for new actions and changes to take place. Remember, being harsh with yourself isn't getting the job done, so why keep doing something that doesn't work? Imagine your young child drops something and breaks it. Would teaching him with kindness be better, or would yelling at him be more effective? The yelling may ensure he doesn't do it again, but that will impact his self-confidence and your relationship with him in the long run. Self-acceptance means that you are just observing the way things are, without judgement. You can now have a choice to take some action to create something better.

How's your practice of self-acceptance going? Are you feeling like you're now able to accept yourself a little bit more? What if you're having trouble with it? What if there's an inner part that's just resisting accepting how things are. Why do you think that is?

One of the biggest reasons why we resist accepting how things are, is because we truly want our circumstances to be another way. The undesirable outcome, however, is that the more we resist, the more things stays the same. This gets us caught in an internal vicious cycle. This is often why you might see someone procrastinating or pushing back on important things, because inside them is a cycle of resistance and rebellion.

Another way we resist situations is that we tell ourselves that something "shouldn't" be this way, or that we just don't want this, but want something else. We might notice that we end up with the same internal conversation for long periods of time because the mind is not designed to respond to negatives such as "don't" and "shouldn't" directly. Instead, it actually has to imagine or visualize that negative action, and then negate it to give us our desired result. So if I tell myself that I don't want to be ugly or fat, my brain will experience what "being fat" feels like, and then aim to negate it. The main issue here is that the image of my being "fat" has been formed, so it might well leave an imprint, at least for some time until a much stronger pattern is formed. This pattern will be one that takes my mind in a completely new and healthy direction. Compare your mind to pencil and paper for a moment. Each time you erase pencil writing on paper, it still leaves a faint mark, so our brain retains a faint mark as well. So what do we do in a situation like this? How do we stop negative imprints from taking hold within our minds and create an empowering self-image?

One of the most empowering ways towards building a healthy self-image is to install an image of the kind of person you truly want to be. Until now, your image of yourself has been largely based on external influences, and now it's time to create a new self-image based on something more internal and constant – and that's values.

What are values?

Are values religious or cultural beliefs? Are they learned or developed? Our values are the motivation behind all that we do. A "value" is something we need to have to feel truly fulfilled. This need is so deep that it drives our very behaviour, whether we are consciously aware of it or not.

Our values are generally established in three big ways. The first is that we have seen the behaviour being enacted over and over. It has been taught to us by a primary carer, so we also start to value it. The second way is that we have missed having it at some point in our lives, and so it becomes a fundamental need. For example, if a Muslim lady has never had the opportunity to speak up in her home growing up, freedom of speech may become a fundamental need for her on leaving home. Without this, she remains unfulfilled. The third way is when we choose to adopt a certain value and establish it in our lives.

Human beings are dynamic, so our values may change depending on our circumstances and what stage of life we are in. However, we will also maintain a set of "core" values that usually remain constant throughout our lives. Our core values drive our behaviour: they compel us to pursue certain careers, live in specific places, and engage with people in unique ways. They are the guiding compass of our life. As a Muslim, Islam forms all your moral and ethical values. Ask yourself, "What does being a practising Muslim give me?" Or ask, "Why do I practise Islam?" You will notice a whole set of values coming up that form your ethical framework. Then ask yourself: What do I need to feel truly fulfilled? You will start to recognize that you need certain things that you didn't have growing up, or you truly long for them to feel fulfilled. For example, freedom of speech, trust, security and so on. Living by all your core values creates a sense of true fulfilment and purpose.

We've defined values as important needs that must be met in order to create fulfilment. Are you wondering how values and self-image are connected? Imagine that you know what you truly want in your life, and how that will help you establish your goals? Imagine that you had a new relationship with yourself, one based on your qualities and capabilities and not external factors, what would that be like? Understanding and eliciting your own values will start giving you access to creating the above scenario. We can begin to build our goals and lives around our values, and secondly, we can create a new image of ourselves and step into that image.

This process needs to take place in two steps. The first step is to elicit your values. This will give you a really good idea of what you truly need in your life. Once you have this awareness, you can then begin to ask yourself who you need to be in order to have what you desire; that's where the constructed self-image comes in. Do the first exercise and begin by uncovering your own core values.

Exercise 3.5: What Are My Core Values?

Outcome: To support you in eliciting your core values. Some of our core values may change from time to time, but most of them tend to remain constant. You can elicit the ones that you feel are more current, and may need to be revisited again.

Method: Draw a wheel of this type in your coaching journal. Answer the questions as you mark the wheel.

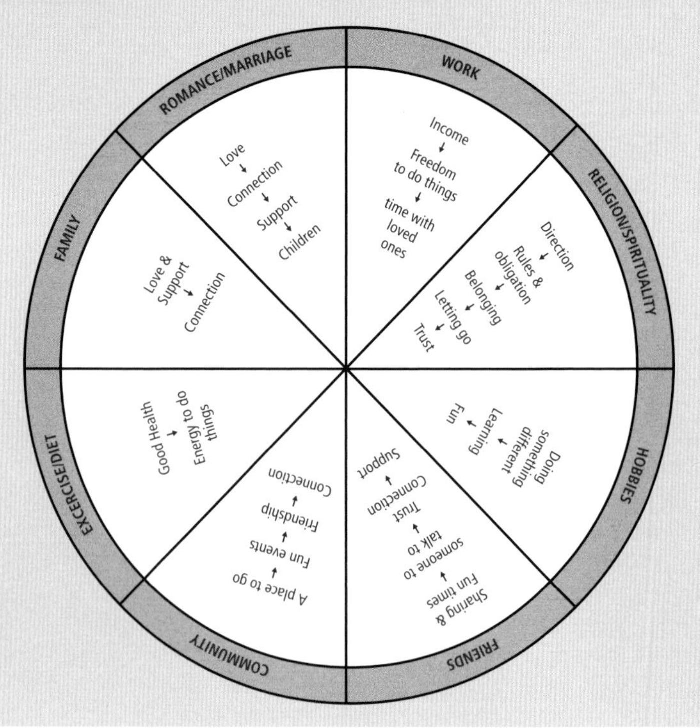

1. Use one piece of the pie to mark each important area of your life. Ask yourself, "what is truly important to me?" You will come up with areas like work, family, religion, recreation and so on…

2. Reflect on ONE area at a time, and ask yourself the questions:

- *"Why is this area important to me?"*
- *"What does it give me in my life?"*
- *What would it be like if I didn't have this in my life?*

Keep asking yourself these questions and unpeeling the layers. For example:

a. What does work give me? *It gives me an income.*
b. What does having an income give me? *It gives me the ability to spend on my family.*
c. What does the ability to spend on my family give me? *It makes me feel as if I'm doing my duty.*

Here, you can dig a bit deeper: is duty the value, or does being dutiful give you something else?

The above is an example. Repeat this process with all the areas that you have chosen.

You will find some value words emerging. Write them down separately.

Observations:

1. What values are you noticing emerging?
2. Which values are so important that they are being reflected through more than one area of your life?
3. Which values were you already aware of?
4. Which ones have come as a surprise to you?
5. Are there any values that are not being met at the moment? What is the impact of that on your life?
6. What did you learn from the previous exercise?

Uncovering our values usually has a surprise or two, and that's a good thing. Now imagine how your choices will be different now that you know what you truly need in your life.

Our values can be thought of as the qualities, that when present, make our lives richer and more fulfilling. For example, if someone values belonging, and they sense that in their lives, then that belonging will help them feel fulfilled. Now that you know what you need, who do you need to be in order to achieve it?

Self-image: Who do I need to be?

We have been trained to think that we need to do certain things in order to get the results we want. We are so focused on all that we have to do that we forget that we aren't human "doings" but human "beings". We might spend our days running from pillar to post, and then feeling completely unfulfilled by the end of it. This would be largely because we didn't spend anytime actually being present to the experience: we were functioning more like machines.

Having awareness of how we're "being" with ourselves and others gives us valuable information. Imagine that you're working towards creating a new business but your body language conveys that you're "being" defeated or negative. Everyone around you will pick up on that energy and you may not achieve your desired outcome. Have you ever had days where you're telling someone you're fine, but you're "being" unresponsive or distant? You might think that the other person doesn't know, but trust me, they do! The way we are "being" has a significant impact on all areas of our lives.

The great news is that you can create a way of being that you truly want. Essentially, this is a whole new self-image. A value-based self-image is an image you have of yourself that is based on qualities that you wish to develop within yourself. You took the first step by exploring your core values. Your values are the qualities that you truly need in your life. Bring your attention to them and explore who you will need to be to successfully emulate these values in your life. Then you can start building a value-based self-image.

Exercise 3.6: Creating a Value-based Self-image

Outcome: To support you in creating a new self-image; one that empowers you to truly live from your values and goals.

Part 1: Exploration

1. Go back and look at the core values exercise. Notice the three that are truly the most important to you. Write them down.

2. Make short notes on:
   a. What would I be saying, doing, and experiencing that would show me that I am living by these values?
   b. What personal characteristics would I need to have to be living from these values? Would I be being loving, kind, courageous, etc?
   c. Imagine that you are living this truly fulfilling life. You have the personal characteristics that you truly want and value. You are living by your three most important core values.

Notice what a day in your life would be like. What would you be doing? Who would you be with? What would your facial expressions and body language be like? Notice each and every detail that you possibly can and write it down. You can start it off by:

"I am living a life I truly want to live, and I can see that I am the person I've always wanted to be. My day begins with...."

Feel free to adapt the beginning if you would like to.

Part 2: Now it's time to visualize

Close your eyes, take a deep breath, and imagine that you are going to a cinema. You enter the cinema, and it is a very small and special cinema. You take your seat. The lights go down and the movie starts. You realize that you are the star of this movie. You are watching a movie called "A day in the life of ___________."
This movie shows an entire day of your life from start to finish.

As you sit in the cinema, make observations about this film as if you were watching any other blockbuster. Notice what the character's body language, facial expressions, and tone of voice are like. Can you tell how empowered this person is? What do you see, hear and experience that tells you that this person has a wonderful self-image? This person is living by what's truly important to them. Things may happen that don't go their way but they accept them because they are living a life by their values. Their image of themselves is based on what characteristics they truly value.

Notice all the action, the colours, and the details of the plot. Notice them walking down the street or interacting with people. Notice all that there is to notice. Just enhance every detail that is noticed.

Now allow your unconscious mind to leave the visualization where it needs to be, and come back to the present moment.

Observations:
1. What did you notice about yourself as the movie was running?
2. How did it feel to see yourself living the qualities you desire?
3. What do you feel is now possible for you?

Take time to run this movie for a minute or two every day. Keep adding in movements and details as you notice them. *Insha'Allah*, over a period of time you will notice that it has become much more effortless to live by those qualities.

Our relationship with ourselves empowers all others

Our relationship with ourselves is lifelong. Once we can truly accept who we are, we can then begin to live by our values and design a self-image that empowers us.

Once you start to value who you are at a deeper level, you will have much more to offer your relationships. The very first thing you will find is that your acceptance and tolerance for others will grow. That in turn will bring room for perhaps love, understanding and greater connections to foster. Remember the oxygen mask example? Once you start to look after your own needs, then you might well have space to take care of others in a meaningful way. *Insha'Allah* the work you have done so far will support your efforts in enhancing the various other relationships in your life. The "self" is truly the foundation of everything that emanates from it. Remember to continue to develop your self-image over time: the stronger it becomes, the greater the chance of fulfilment. You can even start adding your loved ones in there too, as their lives are integrated with yours. Above all, enjoy this journey.

Case Study: Iman's story

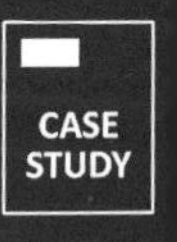

Iman started to come for coaching after taking quite a long time to think about whether she wanted to or not. She had tried so many things, and nothing else had worked, so she decided to give coaching a try. She was a single mum, working in her family business. The main issue that she brought to coaching was her desire to lose weight. She had been struggling for years. She would make some progress, but then would put the weight back on. She described herself as someone who was lacking in discipline and "breaking her diet all the time".

After we started the unpacking process, what really emerged was that her conversation with herself was rather harsh, almost cruel. She would tell herself that "I'm out of control around food." And the words she was using were "loser, failure, ungrateful", etc. When we dug a little bit deeper, it turned out that she hadn't felt comfortable for a long time due to growing up in a different culture. She was trying to make up for being "different" but always failing, and the cycle would continue. Due to her circumstances, she had decided that something was wrong with her. She became stuck in a cycle of setting a harsh target, then blaming herself when she didn't achieve it. After we worked on the subject some more, another theme that emerged was that one of her primary caregivers, her father, had a very harsh demeanour when she was growing up. He was a perfectionist, and according to her, always made her feel less than worthy, that she just wasn't measuring up. This is where she learned her negative self-talk from (one thing to remember is that we often adopt the voice of our primary caregivers. One clue is to notice whose voice it is that we have adopted).

At first, she only wanted to work on habits. Our coaching would revolve around her eating and diet plan, etc. However, both of us began to realize that there was a deeper issue that needed to be addressed. She started to realize that her way of talking to herself would need to change if she was going to get a different result.

She learned to release some of the baggage that was holding her back. Though she still had some way to go, she had learned some productive strategies to soothe herself if her negative self-talk was triggered. She had to learn to separate her own voice about herself from that of her father's. She also learned to set smaller, more manageable goals. She began achieving her targets one by one, and by the end of our time together, she rated herself as far more confident than when she began.

Let's summarise the main points

This chapter addresses the most crucial of all human bonds: the one we have with ourselves. The main idea here was to appreciate the fact that how we deal with others might be a mirror to how we are treating ourselves. When our self-image shifts, our other relationships have a much better chance of succeeding.

- We talked about how often we are compassionate with others, but not with ourselves.
- We explored how our critical self-talk impacts how we feel about ourselves.
- We explored how creating a more compassionate relationship with oneself is useful.
- We defined self-compassion and explored how compassion can soften our self-talk.
- We talked about self-acceptance as a means to enhance our relationship with ourselves.
- So after building some compassion for ourselves, we can then go to the next level by:
  - Exploring what our core values are and,
  - Creating a value-based self-image. A picture of ourselves living how we truly want to live.

4. Enhancing Sibling Relationships

Allah said, "I am the Most Merciful. I created kinship, and I derived it from my name. I will maintain those who maintain it, and I will cut loose those who sever it."

Prophet Muhammad (pbuh)

Is your relationship with a sibling suffering? Are you not speaking? Perhaps you're just exchanging pleasantries. Maybe you've tried to connect, but you've ended up arguing each time, followed by silence for months on end. It feels as if things just always go wrong. Perhaps you're at the point of giving up, but don't do that just yet – have hope. One of the biggest traps that we may fall into is that we think we have done absolutely everything! We even tell ourselves that we are doing something different, but essentially, it's just versions of the same behaviour, and therefore we get similar results. Remember that each behaviour stems from a belief, and, if there's a negative or disempowering belief about any relationship, then that belief will prove itself to be true each time – either through the behaviour, or through the result.

So what is a belief? Essentially, a belief is a thought we have accepted to be the truth, the way "it is". A belief is formed as a response to something such as an event, or things we hear, feel or experience. So when something significant happens to us, we have thoughts about that experience. These thoughts occur within seconds and they are often accompanied by a strong emotion. These specific emotional thoughts are in response to that event – they are the interpretations of that event. Usually one of them is a thought that sticks out, giving rise to an emotion.

Having an initial response isn't the big issue, after all, we need to interpret our experience to make sense of it all. An emotional struggle begins when we have a negative or disempowering belief that dominates. Let's say we have a thought that "my brother is selfish" because he did something that felt that way. Then a second event occurs, and the same thought is repeated. After a couple of similar experiences, we naturally begin to filter out future incidents to collect evidence to prove that he really "is" selfish, and that's the way it is. The thought has turned into a belief.

Over time, enough evidence is collected to turn that thought into a belief. Once we have a thought that we somehow need to hold on to, our minds will filter out experiences to ensure that we can prove this thought to be true. This is how we create most of our beliefs. Let's explore this through another example. Let's say someone has a belief that they are terrible at maths. They are sure that they are terrible at maths. If you ask them how they came to believe this, they will tell you that they were terrible at maths at school. If you were to tease it out a bit more, they would realize that perhaps they had one or two bad experiences with tests or teachers. Those experiences will have had an emotional charge as well. They had negative experiences, perhaps the teachers even said something, or they didn't do well in a test, and that felt quite bad. That whole experience gave rise to the thought that they are "bad at maths".

Once they had that thought, the same thought kept becoming stronger because they kept having issues with other tests and, over time, enough proof was collected to make this the reality for them. Remember that the brain is constantly using past experience to predict what will happen in the future. Given the previous math tests went badly, the brain predicts the same result in the future. This happens enough times and it becomes a firm belief. Remember that this happens with all our beliefs. It's wonderful when we have evidence for all the empowering beliefs we hold, but it can then become equally traumatic when disempowering beliefs start running the show.

Bring your attention to your sibling or siblings now. Just close your eyes and think of each sibling one at a time. How does it feel as you visualize this person? What thoughts are coming to mind? Notice how your own body is feeling. Are you sensing any tightness or discomfort? If so, then there's a high chance that there's some negative emotion, an unresolved issue or a limiting belief in the background. Do the following exercise to get some awareness on what's going on:

Exercise 4.1: What Do I Really Believe About My Sibling?

Outcome: To explore any limiting beliefs that might be impacting your relationship with a sibling.

Method: Just answer the questions below in your coaching journal or notebook. Imagine that I am sitting in front of you, asking you these questions as if we are in a one-to-one coaching session.

First, close your eyes and take three deep breaths. Ensure that you are feeling relaxed, and once you are feeling relaxed and calm, then begin answering the questions:

1. What's the issue in your relationship with your sibling?
2. What are your feelings about him or her right now?
3. Bring your sibling to mind right now, what are your thoughts about him or her?
4. How do you view the situation?
5. Has the situation been like this for a long time, or is this a recent development? If it is recent, can you say what triggered it?
6. What are three things that are true about your relationship with this sibling?
7. How do you know that these things are true?

Observation: *Look at the answers to Questions 6 and 7. What do you notice about them? If they are not actual facts, (such as their age, gender or where they live) then chances are that these are your own beliefs showing up. What we say is true about someone is our set of beliefs about him or her.*

- On a scale of 1–10, how empowering are these beliefs?

1	2	3	4	5	6	7	8	9	10
Not at all									Fully Empowering

- On a scale of 1–10, how possible is it that these beliefs are *your* interpretations of events that have taken place between you?

1	2	3	4	5	6	7	8	9	10

Not at all possible 100% possible

- What is the benefit of having these beliefs?
- What is the cost of having these beliefs?
- Which of these beliefs, if changed, would make the biggest difference to your own level of contentment?
- Is it the same one that is having a negative impact on your relationship with your sibling?
- How would changing this belief enhance the quality of your life?
- Are you now willing to change this belief?

If the answer the last question is a "yes", then proceed to the following. If the answer is a no, then go ahead and write a forgiveness letter (explained in the section regarding resentments) and come back to this later on.

Exercise 4.2: Formulating A New Belief

Outcome: To formulate a new, more empowering belief about your sibling (or about the relationship you have with your sibling).

Step 1: Think of three (or more) new beliefs that you could possibly adopt. Use the fill in the blanks below as possible examples by adding in your sibling's name and completing the thought:
______________________ is caring and wonderful.
My relationship with ______________ is getting back on track.
I am grateful for having ______________________ as my sibling.
I can make a difference to all my relationships in a productive way and having a strong bond with ______________ enriches my life.

Step 1: Looking at the examples above as a guide, brainstorm three (or more) possible new beliefs:

1. ______________________________
2. ______________________________
3. ______________________________

Step 2: Say each one out loud. Notice how each one feels as you speak it out loud. Notice how your body feels, what images come to mind and so on. If you find some tension rising, or it doesn't feel right, then go ahead and brainstorm a few more, until you find one that works. Remember, this is to get the ball rolling, and you can always do this again. And once the baggage begins to be released, your beliefs will automatically begin to shift anyway.

Step 3: Go ahead and choose one belief, and then fill in the blanks putting the whole new belief where the "X" is in the sentence. Example new belief: **"My relationship with _______________ is getting back on track."**

1. X is valuable because I ______________________________
2. X is valuable whenever I ______________________________
3. X is valuable even though ______________________________
4. X is valuable in the same way that ______________________
5. X is valuable so that I can ____________________________

Examples:

My relationship with * Amirah is getting back on track and is valuable because I have missed her.
My relationship with *Waqad is getting back on track and is valuable whenever I think of all our memories together.
My relationship with *Salma is getting back on track and is valuable even though we disagree on many things.

Step 4: Now go ahead and write out your answers by writing the belief at the top and then finishing the sentences so that they make sense. You are creating a short paragraph describing the reasons for your new belief. Follow the example below:

My relationship with Amirah is getting back on track and is valuable: because I have missed her and my relationship with Waqad is valuable whenever I think of all our memories together. My relationship with Salma is getting back on track and that's valuable even though we disagree on many things.

You might find that there are wonderful new reasons to adopt this new belief. If you find that you're not feeling a positive shift, then go back and choose another belief and repeat the above steps. Proceed to the next step once you're feeling that the new belief is working for you.

Tip: You may even replace the word "valuable" with other words such as:
"important", "significant", "cherished", "worthwhile", or any other word that represents significance for you. Feel free to adapt and play with the words to find the one you connect with best.

Step 5: Write your new belief wherever you can see it, so that it serves as a reminder on what you are building. Some ideas are:

- On the bathroom mirror.
- On the fridge.
- On your phone, or computer.
- Near a photo that you can see.

Also use a photo and maybe post these words on it. Use your imagination, but create a powerful reminder with words and images!

Remind yourself of your new belief every day. It will take about 21 days or more of consistent reminding for a new pathway to be formed. A belief is a thought that we believe to be true, so, in time, this new belief will begin to shape your new reality around your sibling.

A bit more about beliefs...

The brain is constantly working to keep us alive and well. The primary purpose of the brain is to do that, isn't it? Thinking is how we interpret all the sensory data that is coming our way in the form of our life's experiences. We experience the world through the body via sight, sound, touch, smell and taste. The thoughts and emotions that the brain creates are aimed to help us to interpret what our bodies are experiencing. We have thousands of thoughts a day, but we don't consciously pay attention to, absorb, nor hold on to most of them – we just couldn't concentrate normally if we did. We do, however, hold on to those thoughts that are somehow relevant to our experience at that given point in time.

The thoughts we tend to hold on to, we do so because they are relevant to us, and our specific life experiences. These thoughts have emotions attached to them, and some of them eventually become our beliefs. This is how we give ourselves an identity and make sense of all the aspects of our lives including ourselves, our relationships and our spirituality. Coming back to siblings and how this all fits together, we need to remind ourselves that any negativity we hold against our siblings is probably due to some beliefs we created after certain specific events. These events may be in the past, but our beliefs are very present in the moment, because the primary function of our brain is to help us to navigate the event should it occur again. This is an automatic, unconscious process and it takes place virtually all the time. Once we have had the same thought pattern occur a few times, our automatic filtering process then takes over and we collect more evidence with each further event.

This must sound and feel bleak, but it's not. The good news is that this process works for all types of beliefs, even the empowering ones. Limiting beliefs look for evidence to keep them strong, and positive beliefs do the same. We don't really think about it, but we have lots of powerful beliefs that may be getting stronger by the day. For example, when friends seek out your company and you feel loved, or when your siblings call and see how you're doing or help you out.

The issue occurs when we have too many limiting beliefs running the show – especially when they are about someone as important as a sibling. It is a vicious cycle that grabs hold of us, unconsciously and can create an internal struggle. On the one hand, our minds are filtering information and finding evidence for what we believe is true, and at the same time the belief itself is suggesting that we look for more evidence. So each time your sibling doesn't call or acts in a way that you think is selfish, you might say, "See, I knew that she's like this, she's done it again!" This cycle can become a never-ending problem and this is why some people break off ties with their siblings entirely.

So what do you do in such a situation? It is truly a no-win situation and the worst part of it is that the biggest battle is within yourself. Indeed, the impact is suffered by all involved, but you have to live with the struggle all the time. The only way out really is to raise one's awareness on what is actually happening. **The very first step is to acknowledge that a belief is a thought, and so just an interpretation of (or a response to) something that happened.** It feels true, there's emotion involved, and we even treat it as if it were a fact. However, if we start to look closely at a belief, we will realize that it isn't a *fact*. Another point for reflection is that we can control which beliefs we hold on to. If a belief is serving us, we should hold on to it, and if a belief is not serving us, we can let it go! It may seem difficult, or even impossible, but what if you could let all the negativity against your sibling go? What would that be like? What would that give you in your own life? How would that enhance the way you're living your life? Focus on that possibility as you go through this chapter because we will be exploring some issues that arise amongst siblings, and how we can handle them better.

We know that our beliefs are essentially thoughts that we hold as truth. Why did we have these thoughts? The simplest answer to this is that these thoughts came about to help us understand certain experiences we had. In summary, something happened, and we had an emotional response to it. That emotion was accompanied with a thought. The point to note here is that the emotion occurs first, and the thought helps give that emotion a name. This near instantaneous process is how we make sense of events. So we have a feeling in the body, and the thought helps us understand that feeling. Our minds put the two together and that becomes our experience.

Let's look at an example to understand this better. You and your siblings are all kids. Your sibling comes and grabs your toy away from you. You feel really bad and you tell your parents. Your parents tell you to let him have it because he's younger. The thought that goes through your mind is that your sibling always gets what he wants. A couple of weeks later, you get a new toy and the same thing happens again – you are now sure that your sibling is always going to get your things. As you are growing older, the pattern keeps repeating where you make forced sacrifices to your younger sibling. Each time this happens, you have the same bad feeling and the same thought to go with it. Over time, the belief that your sibling is selfish has taken hold.

By that point, it is irrelevant that your parents were teaching you to share. What's important is how you experienced that event. All you will have had is past emotional memory, so your experience would filter it with the same lens. So, each time something similar occurred, you reaffirmed the thought you had the first time, and got more evidence for it. This repetition of thought and experience is what forms the belief. The belief will have had simple words when you were a child. As you grew, the same core belief forms layers with more sophisticated words and clusters. However, the essential core belief remains unchanged underneath.

What's the dynamic?

We often have strong beliefs around the family dynamic we grew up in. Looking back, what do you notice about the dynamic that was set up between you and your siblings? How did you and your family members relate to one another? What was it like growing up? Close your eyes, take a deep breath, and recall an important memory from that time. Notice the images, thoughts, and feelings that come up. Once you feel that you've noticed all the important details, you can leave that time in the past, and come back to the present moment.

Write down your observations by answering the following questions:

1. What was the dynamic in my home like?
2. What was my relationship with my siblings like when I was growing up?

3. What are some key things that I am noticing now that I had not noticed before?
4. In what ways did this dynamic contribute to my current relationship with my sibling(s)?
5. What grudges might I still be holding against my sibling(s)?
6. What might I need forgiveness for? Is it a grudge I am holding on to, or something that I did that he or she might be holding against me?

What is opening up from these questions? You probably have some new insights into the dynamic that was formed when you were younger. Is the way that you relate to your siblings still the same, or did it change as you grew older? If things aren't working right now, then now is the time to raise your own awareness of how things got to be this way. It may seem that it's all your sibling's fault, but remember that even he or she interpreted the events that occurred. You have an interpretation, as do they. So if you can look at how you may have contributed to the dynamic, and do something different, then you will most likely get a different result.

Up until now, we were doing some basic preparation work to help you to explore the relationship more deeply. In the following sections, we will talk about some of the specific issues that come up in sibling relationships. Work with the ones that apply to you, and *insha'Allah* you will be able to find empowering ways to improve your relationship.

Issue 1. Jealousy: My sibling always has it all, while I have nothing!

Does your sibling have the kind of life you dream of? Perhaps they have the perfect job, home, spouse and family. Whatever it is, it is what you desire. They have it, and you don't. How does that feel? How has this feeling impacted your relationship? On the surface you have been pretending to be really happy for your sibling, maybe even participating in important events, however, there is a distance between you. There's less conversation, less sharing, and communication is breaking down. Maybe your sibling has even asked you about it, and you've denied it.

Or maybe it's the other way around. Maybe you are the successful one, and your sibling is becoming distant. However, the situation is presenting itself, how are you currently feeling about it?

On a scale from 1–10, how peaceful are you feeling with the situation as it is?

1	2	3	4	5	6	7	8	9	10

Not at all peaceful Completely at peace

Now that we have begun discussing it, let's dig a little bit deeper. Is there a chance that there's some jealousy present? Would it be possible that your sibling feels jealous, or is there a chance that you do? I can appreciate that asking these questions will be upsetting, after all, one should never be jealous of somebody one loves. Just consider the idea that it is an unconscious feeling and not deliberate. And besides that, jealousy is a natural feeling. Just imagine, if things were going really well on both sides, there wouldn't be any jealousy would there? These feelings normally stem from a sense of scarcity, that perhaps we don't have what other people have, and we too want the same things. So let's look at what being jealous means in our context. The way we will define jealousy is:

Jealousy is feeling upset or angry when we notice that another person has something we truly and deeply want for ourselves.

Let's look at this a little more deeply. There's something very important that remains unsaid in the definition, and that is that we feel jealous because *we feel* that we can't have that very thing we want. It's that ***unfulfilled desire*** that's causing the unpleasant feelings, not the fact that we dislike our sibling. Take a moment to reflect – do you dislike your sibling, or that he or she has what you want? Your desires for the having the same things is getting in the way of the relationship. Just take a little while to reflect on this. Now that you've had a little time to digest this idea, it's time to do a short exercise to figure out what you really want, and what might be causing the jealousy.

Exercise 4.3: Reflecting On Feelings Of Jealousy

Outcome: The intended outcome is for you to have more clarity on why you may be having feelings of jealousy towards a sibling.

Method: Answer the questions in your coaching journal. Start with Part 1, and follow the parts depending on which answers come up.

Part 1: Beginning the Enquiry

1. What are the things that my sibling has that I truly want for myself?
2. What would having these things in my own life give me?
3. Why do I really want these things?
4. On a scale of 1–10, how possible is it for me to have these things for myself?

1	2	3	4	5	6	7	8	9	10
Not possible at all									Very possible

Why did I choose the number I chose?

If your answer is below 6, then go to Part 2. If above 5, then go to Part 3

Part 2: If it doesn't feel possible (below 6)

If you feel that it's not really possible, then consider that there is a limiting belief present. To explore this:

1. Why do I feel that it's not really possible for me? Explore the answer to this question. (Is it a fact, or is it something you believe because of past events, or circumstances?)

2. What do I currently sense as true:
   a. About myself around this situation?
   b. About my sibling?
   c. About what's possible for me and my own life?
   d. Which of these beliefs is the one that's impacting me the most?

3. What do I now need to believe instead?

   ____

4. What actions do I now need to take, to start making this belief true?
5. Who might help me?

Part 3: If the answer was 6 or above. Exploring action:

1. Since I believe that these things are possible for me, what actions have I taken so far to realize this possibility?
2. What's worked so far? What do I need to do even better?
3. What is in my control here?
4. Can I make what I need to have happen, happen? (if the answer is no, go back to the exercise on beliefs and explore)
5. Once I have these things in my own life, how will that impact my relationship with my sibling?
6. How might this relationship improve now, as I'm working on these things?
7. How might I seek support from my sibling?
8. What are three new actions that I can now start taking, to make these things a reality in my own life?

   a. ______________________________
   b. ______________________________
   c. ______________________________

Reflection: What have I learned from this exercise? How might I use this learning to improve my relationship with my sibling?

What opened up for you in the previous exercise? What are you now aware of that you were unaware of before? You now had the opportunity to choose – are you going to take some action on having these things for yourself, or are you going to keep things the same? You could continue to hold your sibling responsible, or, instead, you could use his or her success as an incentive – if they can do it, you can do it. This is a moment where you can make a more honest choice. Once you've chosen to work towards achieving this goal, then start setting goals in these areas. If you have worked on it, but circumstances are getting in the way, it might be time to explore avenues for support. Perhaps your sibling may serve as a role model in this regard.

Once you gain some traction, your jealousy should begin to dissipate on its own.

Issue 2. Resentment: My sibling always got his or her way….

Resentment can take hold between siblings, especially if limiting beliefs aren't kept in check. Has there ever been a time when you felt that your sibling was favoured by family more than you were? Perhaps he or she always got their way? Or maybe they did something that was extremely hurtful and you haven't been able to move past it. If we are harbouring some resentments, we first need to understand what resentment truly is in order to transform it. Sometimes, just raising our awareness is enough to resolve the situation.

A definition for resentment is:
Resentment is the anger or ill-will we feel towards someone when we feel that they have been unfair or unkind to us.

1. What has your sibling done that you experienced as being unkind to you?
2. Does your sibling know that you felt his or her behaviour to be unkind?

3. Have you told him or her, or are you assuming that they would know?
4. If your sibling didn't do it, then who did? Is it possible that you are upset with someone else, but taking it out on your sibling?

What's opening up to you here? Did your sibling really do something unfair or unkind? Did he or she do it intentionally? Do they even know that you're hurt? If your sibling is being unfair on purpose, then indeed you're justified in feeling angry. Is that really the case? Or is it that something happened that you interpreted as unfair, and you need for that to be heard and acknowledged.

Feeling resentment is often a sign that you want some acknowledgement of your pain. However, the other person is usually unaware of what you're truly feeling. Another person can't truly feel the same as you're feeling. Also your sibling may not have done anything, and it might be someone else's behaviour you're holding him or her responsible for. We can think of this as resentment by association. It might be that your sister in law said something, but you're upset with your brother because, "He should tell her off."

What if you were able to truly communicate the hurt you're feeling? How would that impact your relationship? What would expressing your hurt give you, and how would it help the relationship? If it wouldn't help the relationship, might it be a better option to just let it all go?

Exercise 4.4: Exploring The Impact Of Resentment

Outcome: To pinpoint the root cause of any resentment you're feeling.

Method: Fill in the blanks and move through the exercise step by step.

Step 1: Stating the complaint. Fill in the blanks below to write down your complaint.

My sibling said or did ________________________ which made me feel really upset, hurt and angry…

I feel that my sibling's behaviour has been unfair to me because

____

Even though my sibling didn't do anything directly, s/he should have

____

My expectation was that my sibling __________________

Step 2: Analysing the impact. Fill in the table with the answers that feel most authentic to you. Remember that this is for you to explore the impact that holding resentment has on your life:

Table 4.1: Exploring the impact of holding resentment

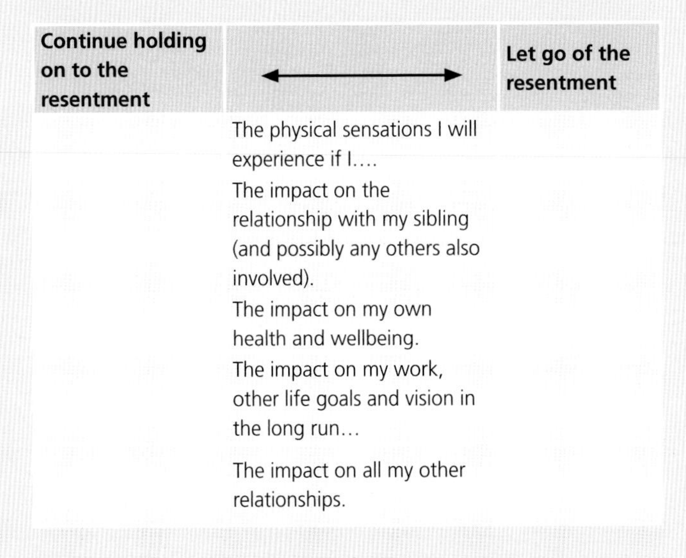

Continue holding on to the resentment	⟵⟶	**Let go of the resentment**
	The physical sensations I will experience if I….	
	The impact on the relationship with my sibling (and possibly any others also involved).	
	The impact on my own health and wellbeing.	
	The impact on my work, other life goals and vision in the long run…	
	The impact on all my other relationships.	

Step 3: Observations. Now take some time to observe what you wrote down, and answer the following questions for yourself.

What I'm noticing from the above exercise is____________________

In summary, the impact of keeping hold of the resentment will be

___

In summary, the impact of letting go of the resentment will be

___

On a scale from 1–10, (10 being the most willing), how willing are you now to release any resentments that you're holding against your sibling:

1	2	3	4	5	6	7	8	9	10

Not at all willing — 100% willing to let it go

If you answer is above 5, then go ahead and move to Step 4. If it is still below 6, then ask yourself, what's stopping you from letting it go. What is the resentment giving you that is so important?

Step 4: Taking practical steps. It's wonderful that you've chosen to let go of the resentment, and now it is time to set a practical strategy in motion to do so. Give the one that appeals to you a try:

1. Write a letter of forgiveness addressed to your sibling. This is a letter for you to air everything that you've been holding back, with the intention of letting it go. Make sure that you state your intention and then talk about what hurt you, and why. Next, write about the new future you wish to have with your sibling. Describe how you want your relationship to be like from now on.

   Caution, it is for the purposes of letting go, so it is not to be shared with your sibling. Once you feel that you've done what's required, then tear it up. And use pen and paper, not a computer. You can repeat this exercise a few times until you feel that the anger has truly dissipated.

2. Practise a gratitude list. Start writing down at least five things that you are grateful for each day. These can be anything from

a good cup of tea, to a chat with a friend. You can do it any time of day you wish. The more gratitude we feel in general, the greater the chance of us feeling happy and being able to forgive the past.

3. Open up a conversation with your sibling: I would recommend that you do this after the forgiveness letter exercise has been completed. Think about the new relationship you wish to develop, and then begin communication.

Once you start letting go of the resentment, you will not only find that your relationship with your sibling improves, but that you have a better quality of health and wellbeing. Give the above exercise a go, and if you still find negative emotions cropping up, then go back and re-do them. Just stay on track and you will get there, *insha'Allah*.

Issue 3. My sibling is always trying to fix me!

We have been talking about family dynamics and issues such as resentment and jealousy can stem from the dynamics that were set up when you were probably much younger. Another issue that can be problematic is if there's a parent–child relationship between siblings, as opposed to a sibling relationship. In certain cases, it may well have been necessary due to significant age difference, but that may not always be the case. Another dynamic could also be that the sibling plays an advisory role all the time, much like a parent, but hasn't done the caretaking part.

Does your sibling start giving you advice, even when you didn't ask for it? How does that feel? On a scale from 1–10, how much do you appreciate it?

1	2	3	4	5	6	7	8	9	10
I dislike it						I really appreciate/ love it			

Where do you find yourself on this scale? What caused you to choose this number? What do you see, feel and experience each time your sibling gives you advice? What would you say is the dynamic between you and this sibling?

Go back and reflect on the time when you were growing up. What role did this sibling play in your life? Take a few minutes to jot down some of the most important memories that you share. Make a note of some of your observations:

Table 4.2: Observing important memories concerning a sibling

Key Event or memory	What happened: What did I do, what did my sibling do?	How did that feel?
The neighbour's son started beating me when I won the basketball game.	She swooped in, grabbed me and protected me from him.	I felt protected, safe.

What are you noticing? What are you noticing about the dynamic of your relationship? Did this sibling play a protective role? How did it feel then? How does it feel now? What's changed? We humans are very interesting in many ways, and one way in particular is that we can slide into old family roles almost instantly – it's actually unconscious and habitual. It is how we are geared to behave. We respond to triggers.

Our trigger–response mechanism is innate and extremely strong: this is how we survive. Actually, it's better referred to as a trigger–reaction mechanism, because we actually react instantly. For example, imagine that there's a car coming at you from the opposite direction, you will swerve to protect yourself. You wouldn't do that only once: you will do that instantly, each time you sense the danger. This is how we respond to triggers. Triggers can be useful or not. For example, an alarm clock is a trigger to wake up or take action.

Our relationships also respond through this same mechanism. One behaviour is a trigger for a reaction. So one sibling's distress is the trigger for the other to respond. This issue only happens when we are so seasoned to respond to that trigger, that we do it instantly, unconsciously, without realizing. So instead of the situation being a trigger, seeing our sibling can be a trigger for how we react. This is why we often react to people in a certain way, even when just thinking about them.

So if your sibling is always giving you advice, or if you feel that he or she is trying to "fix" you, it might just be his or her unconscious response. They may not be meaning to make you feel bad or unworthy, but they may not actually be aware of what's happening. They go into "big brother/ big sister" mode instantly. Another aspect of human behaviour that is interesting to mention is that we are naturally hardwired to fix "the problem". So each time we perceive there is an issue of some sort, we will do our utmost to try to fix it. This is why we experience more people giving us advice than we would like. It can be annoying a lot of the time, but once you are aware that this is a natural human response, it may be easier to handle.

So if you are becoming annoyed with your sibling, or refraining from talking to them, take a moment and just take three deep breaths. Now remind yourself that this may be unconscious and automatic behaviour and not designed to offend you. Once you have taken care of this thought, then you can move forward. One useful way of doing this is to put yourself in your sibling's shoes, so give this a go.

Exercise 4.5: Putting Yourself In Another's Shoes.

Method: This may seem totally bizarre, and I invite you to physically practise this with someone, before aiming to imagine this situation.

Step 1: Ask a friend to help you out with this. Tell your friend that you are just going to follow him or her for a few minutes. Then go outside, and ask your friend to walk about 5–10 steps ahead of you. Observe your friend and try to put your footsteps where they are putting theirs. Observe their gait, and aim to model it. Basically, you are putting yourself in someone else's shoes, without wearing them of course! Walking the way they walk, and looking at the world from their perspective. Stop after five minutes.

Step 2: Now literally give yourself a shake, and notice what you observed. How did it feel to walk that way? What did you notice about the environment or anything else, from someone else's perspective?

Step 3: Now visualize this with your sibling. Sit down in a quiet space where you will be undisturbed. Close your eyes and imagine yourself with your sibling, perhaps you are doing something together. Now imagine that you are leaving your body, and observing the situation from a distance (either above or to the side). As an observer, notice the interaction between you and your sibling. What are you noticing about how you both interact? Is your sibling giving you advice? Notice what might be motivating this. Notice other details such as body language, actions and anything else you see. Once you feel that you have a keen sense of what the situation is, then go ahead and open your eyes.

Write down your observations:
I now see that my sibling gives me advice because__________________________________
I sense that his/her intention is to ______________________
Now that I see this, one way that I can respond differently is to
____

What did you observe and learn from the previous exercise? You may have noticed that the motivation on both your parts is positive, but the interaction isn't very productive at present.

Remember that **every human being has a unique model of the world** and that your sibling has positive intentions. So how do you handle such a situation? You don't want to alienate or hurt your sibling, yet you don't want advice all the time either. So here are a couple of tips to get something different started:

1. Notice if you are constantly reaching out to your sibling when you have an issue. It might be time to refrain once in a while. Share once you have handled it, not before.
2. Do something new and fun together – engage in a way you haven't done before. Allow him or her to see a different side of you.
3. Set up an easy code word together. When you experience your sibling going into advice-giving mode, then just speak the code word. For example, "Big sister mode".
4. Get into dialogue. You might find that he or she knows that they are giving you advice, but hadn't realized that you didn't want it. Let them know that you will openly request it when you need to, and they are still wanted in your life!
5. The next time he or she goes into advice-giving mode, just remind yourself that its habit. Take three deep breaths, move away for a moment if you need to, and then respond in a kind but honest manner. Say what you need to say and request your sibling to allow you to sort out your own concerns at this time.
6. Tell him or her in advance, that you just want to share, not to fix!

My sibling isn't giving advice, he is bossing me around!

Do you feel dominated by your sibling? Does he or she always tell you what to do, or perhaps doesn't really take no for an answer? This doesn't feel like advice does it? Some of us may be in situations where we work with our siblings, or are closely dependent on them in other ways so it becomes difficult to stand up for ourselves or say no. The fear of financial fallout or other issues can play a huge role in not standing up for ourselves. But, just imagine, if you keep going this way, how will you be feeling in the next five years? Ten years? Or even twenty? What might happen if you allow things to stay the same? What's the risk here?

Perhaps you feel that no matter what you try, you always lose. Your sibling has the upper hand, and may even throw a tantrum when they don't get their way. We may feel trapped in such situations, not knowing what to do. Indeed, it's not a one-size-fits-all approach. Now it may sound like I'm adding to the hopelessness, but the aim is not to do that. Keep doing different things till you figure out what works. Another hint, there may be a limiting belief lingering underneath, so look into that as well by working on the first exercise. We may think that we only have one limiting belief, and we have sorted it all out, but if something that tugs at us comes up again and again, then chances are that there are other limiting beliefs underneath. So go back and explore what the belief around your sibling might be.

Also here is another exploration:

Exercise 4.6: Focusing On What I Can Influence:

Outcome: To support you in noticing which behaviours are in your own control, and keeping your focus on those.

Method: The questions and table as laid out.

Part 1: **Exploration.**
What are the behaviours that I am finding difficult to deal with?
How am I currently reacting to those behaviours?
Even though my reactions feel justified, are they helping the situation?
If not, then what are some things that I can change? How might they impact the situation positively?

Take some time to also note down what is in your control, or not in your control. Use the following table as a guide:
The situation between my sibling and myself is that

____

Table 4.3: Exploring control

What are the thoughts, feelings and behaviours that are **not** in my control?	What are the thoughts, feelings and behaviours that **are** in my control?

Part 2: **Observe.**
Where is your focus most of the time? Is it on the things that you control, or on the ones that are not in your control?
What is one thing that is "in your control" that you can focus on, to make a productive shift in the situation?

Part 3: Exploring new opportunities for action.
Write down up to three ways in which to make this possible:

1. ______________________________
2. ______________________________
3. ______________________________

We might be tempted to "**fix**" our sibling, or ask someone else to do this for us. Unfortunately, we can never fix anyone else, nor can we change them. We can only change and shift our response to what is happening – the great news is that shifting our response is often what's needed to shift the dynamic!

Issue 4. Competition/rivalry: My sibling is always trying to get "one up" on me

This might be one of the most common issues among siblings, and even more so with siblings of the same gender. Do you feel that your sibling is always in competition with you, trying to get one up on you in some way? How does that feel? People who experience this with their siblings do tend to feel angry and frustrated. Every situation, good or bad, somehow becomes about their sibling. Sound familiar?

There is also the flip side to this dynamic. Do you feel that you don't measure up against your siblings? Perhaps that your siblings are better than you, and they always show it. Maybe one of them always makes you feel bad about where you fall short, or taunt you in some way. This is primarily to hurt you, or compete in some way. One example I came across is of two sisters. They are about a decade apart in age, both are successful in their careers and live on two different continents. They do however, have a significant age difference between them. One more thing to note is that one of them, the younger one, has an issue with her weight. While they were growing up, the older one would always chide the younger one calling her fat. This taunting has impacted her a great deal. We don't really know exactly why the older one was doing this, but rest assured a dynamic was set up, which is continuing till today.

The only way that we can shift something, is to explore our own situation and get some freedom around it. We will separate this sibling rivalry into two main groups. Work with the situation that best fits what you are facing.

Situation 1: My siblings are smarter, prettier, and well, just better than me

Did you experience your parents comparing you and your siblings to one another? Many times, this is the beginning of this kind of competition. One sibling is often compared to another, and the one whose being told this is usually the one that doesn't measure up somehow. This eventually leads to beliefs and feelings of inadequacy. Go back to the first section on beliefs and I invite you to look for those feelings where you felt inadequate in comparison to your sibling. Bring up that situation or memory, and ask yourself:

"What did I decide in that moment?"
"What did I believe about myself? Do I still believe this?"
"What did I believe about my parent?"
"What did I believe about my sibling?" Do I still believe this?"

Ask these questions one at a time, and you might begin to notice some limiting beliefs popping up. Go ahead and do the beliefs change exercise, on the belief that has the most impact on you. You might notice a belief that is a comparison, but you can make the belief just about yourself. For example:

Limiting belief: "Everyone always likes her more than they like me; she's the favourite".

New Belief: "I am my own person with my own strengths and things to offer."

These are just a couple of examples so that you can get a reference point of what you're looking for. One of the biggest issues that we need to deal with in relation to sibling rivalry is to actually become aware of the competition that was created, and then shift it. This is not about blaming the situation, parents, or even our siblings. This is about creating awareness around the dynamic that existed, and now working towards shifting the dynamic to a more empowering one. Once you feel that you have a new belief that feels good, then write it down and put it as a reminder where you can see it. Put it up on your bathroom mirror, in your room, phone or computer. Each time you see it, say it to yourself and take a moment to connect with this new belief.

You will have taken the first step towards a more empowered you when you shift a belief. For the belief to stick, you need to find new evidence for that new belief. One of the best ways in which we can do that, is to start looking towards our own strengths and achievements. Below is a simple exercise that will support you in finding powerful evidence for your own successes.

Exercise 4.6: Focusing On Your Strengths

Outcome: To start to notice your own strengths and achievements.

Method: This is a simple exercise. You will be working with your coaching journal for this. Start with a new page each time, and take a few minutes to list down everything you did well, or accomplished during the day. It need not be big things, everything small and big, counts. From saying prayers, to making a good meal or dropping the children off. List it all.

After thirty days, go back and look at the pages for the month. You will notice how many things you actually do well. This is who you are, and what you are doing with your own life, begin to notice all the new evidence that is in line with your new belief.

Situation 2: My sibling is always competing, trying to get one up on me

Think back to when you were younger. Did you have more privileges at home than your sibling? Did you do better in school, or have more opportunities come your way? There's no reason to apologize for any of that, but how do you now think that it might have impacted your sibling? Did your parents use your achievements as a reference point for a sibling? What are you noticing now that you hadn't before?
Now that you might have some new awareness about the past, let's move to the present. It is important to keep this in mind: with awareness comes change. Your sibling might be annoying or be frustrating you, but as we mentioned earlier, there is always a reaction to a trigger. One possible way to shift the dynamic is to shift how you respond to the trigger. So let's begin this process by raising your awareness on what you might do differently the next time your buttons get pushed:

Exercise 4.7: Understanding The Trigger To Sibling Competition

Outcome: To support you in noticing how you might respond differently to any "trigger" behaviours from your sibling.

Method: Bring specific events to mind when your sibling did or said something that you felt was competitive. Notice what your sibling said or did, and how you reacted. Notice the impact of that reaction. Now is the opportunity to notice how you might "respond" differently in order to shift the dynamic.

Table 4.4: Shifting the dynamic between you and your sibling

What my sibling did: Something that "felt" competitive and "triggered" me.	How I currently react when s/he does this. What should I do?	What is the impact? On me? On my sibling? On the situation?	How might I respond differently?	What might help me to remember this new behaviour?

You have come up with some possible new behaviours so give yourself ample opportunity to practise them. Put some reminders where you can see them. Reminders are wonderful because we can then free ourselves up to think about other things. Put a "bell" or ding on your phone, or you can put up the words where you can see them – anything that will remind you to respond the next time something triggers you. Again, you can practise these behaviours with other people as well, not just your sibling.

Observations after thirty days

After a month of practising the new behaviours, take some time to do an audit. Figure out which ones are working and which ones aren't. This observation part is essential if you are going to make changes that will last. If something is not working, then ask yourself, "What might I do instead?"

A great way of telling whether your new behaviours are working is the impact on the relationship. Notice what changes are occurring. Are you getting along better? Are you able to spend more time with your sibling without feeling reactive, irritated or upset? Noticing your own emotional and physical wellbeing is the most accurate way of assessing whether the change is working or not.

There are often opportunities to try out something new right in front of us, but we may not see them because we are blocked by limiting beliefs, or doing what we've always done. Once we approach the situation with fresh eyes, a lot can open up, and transformation becomes possible!

There are various other dynamics that we probably did not touch on. If there is any situation that is specific to you, but not mentioned here, think about it with fresh eyes. You will notice that you can apply some of the same exercises to your specific situation. Give the exercises a go, and just be willing to raise your awareness. New insights and opportunities for action will emerge, *insha'Allah*.

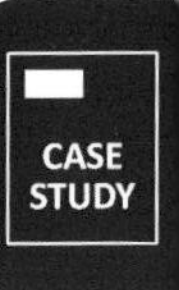

Case Study: Ameena

Ameena was in her twenties when she came to coaching. She was doing well in her career, but her family life was the main issue. She was single and living at home. Her father had passed away some years ago. Her older brother, who was married, had assumed responsibility as head of the household. The main issue that Ameena wanted to address was that she and her brother were not speaking. They had been living under the same roof, but not spoken directly in over a year. This was due to the fact that her brother was upset because she had given up her studies to be a doctor, and had pursued an alternative career.

Though quite happy with her choice, Ameena was feeling bullied and controlled by her brother. There was a lot of blaming between them, and we knew that her brother would not come to coaching. She thought her brother was just being dominating and forcing his will on her. It was clear to me that she loved her brother, otherwise it wouldn't have been such a huge issue for her. She had a good relationship with other household members too.

Up to the time she began coaching, Ameena had just accepted the situation as it was. She wasn't sure what to do, because she had tried to talk to him, but he had been unwilling. She couldn't really understand what the "big deal" was.

Through the coaching process, Ameena began to step into her brother's shoes a little bit. She started to consider the idea that that maybe her brother felt responsible for her wellbeing, having assumed the role as father figure. He might have felt pressure to fulfil his father's wishes, and so was then putting pressure on his sister. It had been her father's wish that she become a doctor like he was. In fact, she had begun the admission process while her father was still alive. The whole family was excited that she would follow her father's footsteps.

Ameena began her medical degree, and got through the first year. But she realized that she just didn't want to do it any longer. She gave up the course without telling her brother and pursued another internship.

Now, that she was happier in her new direction and had gotten herself a good job (she was working for a politician), she really wanted to open up communication with her brother. Through coaching she learned to give up the resentment that she was holding against him. Over time, she made requests to start talking, and by the time she concluded her coaching, she and her brother had begun speaking. There was work ahead, but they had opened the door to a more forgiving and understanding relationship.

Let's summarise the main points

- We explored what beliefs are.
- We explored how to shift a limiting belief and form a new, more empowering one.
- We explored the concept that family roles and dynamics are often formed when we are young.
- We looked at different issues that crop us between siblings.
- We looked at various exercises and tools to raise our awareness, so that we can enhance sibling relationships.

5. Parenting: Creating Love and Joy in the Relationship with Our Kids

Your possessions and your children are only a trial, and Allah it is with Whom is a great reward. Therefore be careful of (your duty to) Allah as much as you can, and hear and obey and spend, it is better for your souls; and whoever is saved from the greediness of his soul, these it is that are the successful.

Qur'an 64:15–16

Verily, all of you are shepherds and all of you are responsible for your flocks.

Prophet Muhammad (pbuh)

Is parenting the hardest job in the world?

I would personally answer that question with a resounding yes! You have a very tough job as a parent, but your kids have a very tough job too. Kids have parents, grandparents, teachers and extended families all telling them what to do. They have to learn about social skills, religion, school, and they also have to learn how to deal with friends, find their place amongst their siblings, and try to get their parents' attention. It is a **lot** for them!

So whether you are conscious of it or not, your kids have a lot going on. And it's very frustrating for them when they really want something, but they can't have it because their parents' control what they can have. No one likes being bossed around all day long – just imagine how you would feel if that was happening to you now?

But you have the tough job of preparing your kids for life ahead. This means that you are compelled to do whatever it takes to make this happen, right? However, your children may not always co-operate with all the things that you need them to do. This leads to power struggles, nagging, and other negative behaviours – you're probably no stranger to those.

But what if you could get your kids to co-operate, and get them to do the things you need them to do? After all, it is for their own good isn't it? Do you succeed by nagging, arguing, and having power struggles?

Think about the last time that you yelled at your child. How did you feel afterwards? How do you think your child felt? When everyday situations turn into power struggles, no one wins. You would have felt guilty, and your child will have had another negative experience of you. You don't want your children to dislike you, or end up feeling small or insignificant, do you? No wonder being a parent is so difficult – you have to teach your children, but they may not always be willing!

Just reflect on the last negative interaction you had with your child. What was your emotional need in that moment? Take a moment to reflect on what it was. Your need motivated your behaviour and you may not even have been aware that this was happening. What did your child need emotionally in that moment? Maybe your child wanted to do what he or she wanted, but behaviour is motivated by emotional needs to a much greater extent than just that particular moment. So even when behaviour seems unreasonable or negative, it is motivated by the desire to have a certain need met. This is the same for children and adults.

Now, I'm not at all suggesting that we let our children do whatever they want, just because they have emotional needs, in fact, just giving in may not even meet the very need they have. I'm suggesting a different idea altogether.

When a parent understands what the child's emotional needs are, and fulfils those emotional needs on a regular basis, then the child's behaviour will improve and training him or her for life will become a lot more enjoyable for both.

In this chapter, we will put our focus on understanding what children need emotionally. We will also explore tools that help us, as parents, to meet these needs for our children.

What is your parenting style?

Let's face it, none of us has perfect children. Our children will throw tantrums, be naughty, not listen to directions, or just plain defy us. Many parents often feel challenged by their children. I've heard so many parents say that, "Oh, all kids are like this nowadays." What is it about this generation of kids that makes them so much more challenging than you were?

Consider that it is **not** your child who is to blame. Consider that your own parenting style is often responsible for how your kids react. Just reflect on how you were parented for a moment. Did you grow up in the generation when **"kids were meant to be seen, but not heard?"** Were you ever yelled at by a person twice your size? How did it feel? We often parent the way we were parented, because we inadvertently do what we know. Did you ever promise yourself that you will never parent like your parents – and now catch yourself doing the same thing? This is natural, we do what we know! But there's hope. In order to make a change, you will first need to become aware of how we parent now, so you can then go ahead and do something about it. Now is the opportunity to begin raising awareness on how you might be parenting. So go ahead and work on the following exercise to start the process.

Exercise 5.1: Parenting Awareness Questionnaire

Desired outcome: To raise your awareness on how you are currently parenting.

Method: Answer the following questions with the most accurate response reflecting how you would most likely act. Make a quick choice and use your instincts. Don't overthink or second guess yourself here.

1. **Your child is throwing a tantrum at the shop because she just saw her favourite cookies on the shelf, and she wants to have one right now. You say no, because you have some at home.**

People are staring at you, and are getting annoyed by your screaming child. Do you:

a. Pick up a bag, open it, and let her have one?
b. Take her by the hand, and say that, "I know you would like to have it now, but we have some at home, and you can have one after dinner"?
c. Pick her up, go to a quiet corner, or outside, and wait for her to calm down, until you are ready to continue shopping? Or
d. Yell at her, "Stop crying right now or you won't get a cookie for another week!"

2. **You are at home doing housework. You hear your children fighting over a toy. Suddenly they both come to you saying, "He hit me." or "She started it." Do you:**
   a. Mumble: "I wish these kids would just get along for once," and then attempt to pacify them both?
   b. Listen to the details, and discipline the one who you think needs it?
   c. Ask them to work it out amongst themselves?
   d. Send them both for a time out, and tell them there's no screen time tonight?

3. **You have a teenager. You walk into his room, and as usual you see everything all over the place. Do you:**
   a. Take a deep breath and start cleaning his room?
   b. Sit down with your child, explain that this mess is unacceptable, and ask him for suggestions on how to keep his room clean?
   c. Tell him, "I am leaving your room now, and I expect it to be cleaned up before dinner"?
   d. Grab a trash bag, and start throwing all his stuff in there, as you've had enough, and he's going to have to suffer the consequences?

4. **Several of your 17-year-old son's friends have tattoos. Your son wants to get one. You do not agree with this for several reasons. Do you:**

a. Say no, but you are sure that he will do it anyway?
b. Say no, but he keeps asking every day. He promises that it will only be a small one, that will be on his shoulder where no one can see it. He promises he will show you the design and it will be tasteful. You say "Okay" because you know you can't win them all?
c. Tell him that you don't like the idea and give him your reasons why. You then tell him to make his own decision?
d. You absolutely forbid it and threaten to ground him for a month?

5. Its 11:30pm and your child is sleeping. It was her responsibility to feed the cat, and she has forgotten to do it yet again. Do you:

a. Feed the cat, as you usually end up doing?
b. Feed the cat, and use breakfast time to explain what it means to have a pet?
c. Feed the cat that night, but you sit down with her to create and implement a plan for feeding the cat. You also lay down a consequence if it's not done?
d. Wake your daughter up yelling, "Go feed the cat, I'm tired of doing it for you"?

Scoring: Give yourself:

1 point for each A
2 points for each B
3 points for each C
4 points for each D

What your scores might mean:

1–8 Points: The Indulgent Parent

Do you often say yes to things just to avoid tantrums or to keep the peace? Are you finding it difficult to say no? Does this leave you feeling frustrated or angry at times? Indeed, it is extremely difficult to deal with power struggles, and this style of parenting might work in the moment, but it doesn't prepare children to deal with the disappointments of life. When we keep saying yes to things, our children don't really learn how to deal with any refusals or challenges that will come down the line. They also might be getting an unconscious message that tantrums are an acceptable strategy to get what they want. Use some of the tips and strategies in this chapter to support you in creating clearer boundaries and rules for your children.

8–12 Points: The Teaching Parent

You may well be having some success in gaining your child's co-operation, but you spend a lot of time explaining things. You're always trying to be fair and reasonable, and deal with tantrums as a teacher would. However, there are times when you may also feel tired of the struggle, or just unable to get through. There are some skills in this chapter that are just about "being" with your child, and you may notice opportunities to "be" more, and explain less.

12–16: The Balanced Parent

Are you reading parenting books, or maybe taking classes? You are probably getting really good results with your kids, and you are learning how to meet their emotional needs. However, are there times when you are just really hard on yourself? Maybe you're pushing yourself to be perfect? There is no such thing as a perfect parent, so continue learning, but be kind to yourself as well.

16–20: The Controlling Parent

Is it your way or the highway in your house? Did you grow up with very strict parents yourself? How did it feel? What impact did it have on your sense of self-esteem and autonomy? Indeed, you may be running a tight ship, but exerting extreme control can also have a very damaging effect on the parent–child relationship. Consider that there may be times to enlist your child's co-operation without having to lay down the law, or being overly strict. We will be talking about what children really need, and how you can gain more co-operation while nurturing your relationship as well.

There is no perfect test to figure out what kind of parent you are. Parenting is learning by trial and error. The above questionnaire has been offered to raise your awareness as a general guideline. Please do not consider it a definitive test. If the answers feel as if you can relate to them, then go ahead and use them as a guideline to look for potential areas of improvement. If you feel that you have a mix of all the styles, that's fine too. just take this as an opportunity to raise your awareness of what you're already doing well, and what you may be able to do even better.

Why do your kids misbehave anyway?

This is an important question, but let me begin by asking you: why do adults lose their temper when they do? Have you ever lost your temper? Recall the event and ask yourself what caused you to do that. Was someone not listening to you? Were you feeling unable to get through? The reason why adults become angry, or yell is because one of their important needs is being overlooked. Children are similar to adults in this way.

Children misbehave because their emotional needs are not being met in positive ways, and so they are resorting to other behaviours to have that need met.

If a child is not able to meet a need in a positive way, he or she will do what "works" in order to have that need met. Now this is not planned or malicious on the part of any human being – adult or child – we operate instinctively in these situations.

One important need for a child is attention. Imagine that you are on the phone, your child has tried to get your attention for several minutes, but with no luck. He or she keeps trying to get your attention until you finally yell, "Just give me five minutes, can't you see I'm on the phone?" leaving your child feeling shocked and hurt. What happened here? Your child was not trying to be bad or annoy you, he just needed a little attention, but didn't know how else to get the attention he needed, other than in the only way that he knew how. Children have very specific emotional needs, and when those needs are met, parents will get more co-operation, less tantrums, and a more enjoyable parenting experience overall.

So what are the most important emotional needs that kids have?

Think of a recent moment when your child was really excited. Maybe she got an A on a test, or perhaps she was able to do a chore all by herself, and all she wanted to do was to first share it with you. Our children get a wonderful boost in confidence when they are noticed for something that they have done well – it does wonders for their confidence! This is because our acknowledgment meets one of the two more important emotional needs that children have.

The two most important emotional needs for a child are to feel that he or she is a valued member of the family, and that what he or she wants matters. These can be defined as the need for connection and the need to experience personal influence, or positive power in the relationship.

If we reflect, we will notice that even adults have these same needs. Adults are able to recognize their needs and request for them to be met. Children, however, are not able to articulate their needs, so parents need to be proactive to recognize them, and consciously work towards meeting these needs for their children. As a parent, when you do this, you will notice the tantrums and power struggles calming down, as you and your family all experience a much more fulfilling family life. So let's talk about these needs a little bit more.

A child's need for connection means that he or she feels a strong need to belong within the family. When the child knows how he or she fits in with his parents and siblings, and can feel secure within the family, then this need for connection is being met. When children feel that they belong within the family, it is easier for them to recognize what belonging looks like with their friends, and at school. Any adult can empathize with this, as adults also need to experience connection with their loved ones, friends, and colleagues.

The need to feel positive power is equally important, and this is one which parents may unconsciously overlook. **A child's need for positive power means that he or she needs to feel that he or she is capable in various ways, including contributing to the family, and has some control over his or her life as well.** Human beings have an innate need to feel free. Children, even though they are not yet independent, still have the need to feel that they have some control over their lives.

Do I disempower my kids?

No one is more well-meaning than a parent. We want our children to excel in every way. However, we may, unintentionally, disempower our children by subtle things we do. But before I give you some examples, take a moment to reflect on your own parenting style. If you are an indulgent parent, how might always saying "yes" impact your children's need for power and connection? What might be the benefits or the disadvantages? Take a moment to ask yourself the following questions.

1. How is my parenting style impacting my child's need for connection and positive power?
2. What do I see, hear, and experience in my child's behaviour that tells me this?
3. What is it that I'm doing to meet my child's needs?
4. How might I be disempowering my child (while not meaning to)?
5. What is one behaviour towards my child that I intend to change?

Parents have a lot of influence on their children's feelings and behaviour. Let's look at some of the common and subtle ways that parents take away their children's sense of personal autonomy and / or connection. What are parents sometimes guilty of?

Being sarcastic: Even as a joke (the child feels mocked – think about how you react to sarcasm).

Expecting perfection: Imagine your child comes home with a B+ that she worked really hard on, and the first thing you say is "Why isn't this an A?" This really hurts their sense of capability, and makes the child feel that they can never be good enough.

Discussing a problem that the child is facing (with another adult) in front of them: Makes them feel embarrassed, and not good enough.

Nagging: Sends the message that you don't trust them to be capable enough to remember simple things.

Labelling them: For example: my smart child, my difficult child, my messy child, etc. The child is boxed in, and forced, unconsciously, to live by that label.

Comparing: To siblings, friends, other children. "I wish you would be more like X." This behaviour is all too common and is a cause of sibling rivalry as the child doesn't feel "as good" or much a part of the family as the other child.

Choosing everything for them: There are times when it's okay for a child to have a choice. By robbing a child of that opportunity, he or she feels powerless, and he or she is not able to learn how to make choices for himself or herself.

There are some obvious ways in which parents disempower their children. These include:

Hitting: Imagine being hit as an adult, how would that feel? Children feel equally violated, but they don't have the power to defend themselves. This also sends the message that the parent has lost all control and is unable to handle the situation.

Yelling: Screaming sends the message that it's okay to scream at someone if they don't comply. It makes children feel afraid, and powerless to get their point of view across.

Do any of these behaviours feel familiar to you? Don't worry if they do – the idea is to raise your awareness and make a change. We all do the best we can, and remember, children don't come with a manual, so all you can do is learn, and make one positive change at a time. Throughout the rest of this chapter, we will explore some small tools used to fulfil the needs of connection and positive power for our children. Give the tools a try and see which ones work best for you. *Insha'Allah* you will experience parenting in a whole new way – with a more loving, and enjoyable environment in your home.

Tools to build connection

Spending Quality Time

Do you remember the last time you spent real quality time with your children, just doing what they loved? How did that time impact you? How did your children feel? The most impactful thing we can do for our children is to spend quality time with them. So what does this mean for our kids? It means that:

- We are doing something that **they** love to do.
- We are giving them our **full** attention: we are available emotionally and physically (no distractions).
- We are not teaching, preaching, nagging or yelling – this time is just for fun and bonding.

How do you do this?

- Take out 10–15 minutes of time for each child each day. You can increase it to twice a day if possible. Or, each parent can have one chunk of time a day.
- Spend this time with each child individually (meaning one-to-one, one parent and one child).
- Do something that your child loves to do.

This time will do wonders for your child's need for connection. You will also feel wonderful – after all, you get to spend some time being a kid!

Quality Listening: Create a Safe Space

How much time do you spend **listening** to your kids instead of talking to them? Many parents think that they are listening, but in reality, they end up talking a lot more than listening. This is not because they don't want to listen, but they are probably acting out of fear. Parents are afraid that their kids are going to do something wrong – so we go into lecturing mode without realizing it. This can be very unproductive because kids start to zone out each time they sense a lecture coming.

Have you ever seen your child roll his eyes and just stand there? There's an empty look on his face, and he's pretending to listen. He actually tuned your voice out a long time ago. You probably know that he's tuned you out, but you keep going. Even if you escalate your tone, you will have to keep raising your voice, or do something drastic to get his attention, and when you do, it doesn't end well does it?

So why do our children tune us out when we are trying to explain something to them? This is because we are not having a two-way dialogue. Instead, we are talking "at" rather "to" them. So how do we get our kids to listen to us? This might sound crazy, but the way to get our kids to listen to us, is if we truly listen to them! Just imagine that you have someone in your life who is always trying to "fix" you. How does that feel?

Our children don't want to feel that they need "fixing". Many parents complain that their kids don't talk to them, but have they wondered why? Do they try to fix things, or do they provide a safe space?

A safe space is experienced when someone is able to share without fear of judgement, criticism or correction.

Just imagine what it would be like for your child to know that he or she can talk to you about anything, without having to worry that you'll get angry, or react in a negative way. You may have told your kids to come and talk to you, but if they don't experience that sense of safety they won't open up. This is easier said than done because it's your job to teach your kids and protect them from this big bad world out there – but it is a delicate balance between when to be in "parent" mode, and when not to be. So let's talk about the options of how you can "be" something else instead.

There's a model used in modern psychology called "transactional analysis". It was developed by a Canadian psychiatrist named Eric Berne. Berne said that people function from one of three ego states at all times, and they move between these states in different situations. You can look into his theory further, but we will talk about it here in the context of communicating with our kids.

1. The "Parent" Ego State: This is when we are teaching, directing, or telling our kids what to do. Our stance is that of a teacher, and of someone in authority. It can be a highly emotional state, especially if we are angry at or upset with the child.

2. The "Adult" Ego State: This is when we are communicating as an adult, and we are mostly in this state when we are interacting with our peers, or with other adults in general. We are less emotional and are able to communicate with ease and comfort.

3. The "Child" Ego State: This shows up when we are playing with our children – remember the last time you just had child-like fun with your kids? This is the state that most young children are in all the time. This is a highly emotional state, and this is the same state as when a child (or adult) is having a tantrum.

Which state would you need to be in to provide a safe space for your child? It would be the "adult" way of being. Just imagine that you can listen to your child, without trying to fix anything – just giving him or her space to sort things out without pressure. When he needs advice, he will be able to ask you himself. So let's look at some tips on how to listen deeply, and create a safe space.

1. Ensure that you can suspend **"parent"** mode for a while. Remind yourself that this is time to just allow for your child to speak; the teaching can come later.
2. Avoid forcing the issue. Just "be" present and available. Allow your child to speak when they are ready.
3. Minimize distractions.
4. Adopt a curious mindset. Think that this is an opportunity to get to know your child better. You may notice the urge to "fix" coming up, just notice it, and let it go.
5. Notice your child's body language, and tone of voice. This will give you cues as to what's happening at a deeper level.
6. Reassure your child that you will not get upset or try to fix the situation – that you are just there to lend an ear.

Notice what happens when you start spending quality time with your child *and* listening to what your child is trying to say. Focus on one skill at a time. With conscious practice, your listening skills will improve.

Use the 5–1 Rule of Thumb

Many parents, especially those who have older children, often have more negative parent–child interactions than positive ones. Imagine if you were on the receiving end of nagging, yelling, or comparing most of the time? How would that leave you feeling? Would you feel wounded, maybe

even confused? Negative interactions with our children impact them a great deal; in fact, we don't even know what the lasting effect of these interactions will be. So does this mean that you can never discipline your children? Of course not, but it does matter **how** you do it. Consider that any interaction where a child is hit, yelled at, humiliated, or in any way made to feel small is a negative interaction. A positive interaction, on the other hand, is any interaction that fosters feelings of connection between you, offers the child some learning, and positive power. Even discipline, if done appropriately, can be a "positive" interaction in this sense.
So how do parents reduce the number of negative incidents?

The general rule to keep in mind is that it takes five positive interactions to overcome the impact of each single negative interaction.

1. Record your interactions

Start documenting your interactions for a few days. Just post a piece of paper on the fridge (or wherever you have easy access). Make two columns, label one "positive" and label the second "negative". Just make a line or a dot after each interaction in the appropriate column. Use any system that works for you – this is not about documenting the details of the interactions, but just to get an idea of **how many, and in what category**. After about a week or so, you will get an idea of whether you are having more negative or more positive interactions with your children.

This awareness will help you shift your focus towards having more positive interactions with your children. You may even start catching yourself in the middle of yelling – giving you a choice in the moment!

2. Practice acknowledgement

Do you want your kids to be the best at everything they do? Are you always pushing them (and even yourself) to do better? Just imagine that your child comes home from school, and she looks a little down. She had a biology test this week, and she reported that it was really hard. You ask about the test, and she shows you the graded paper – it's a C. How do you react? Do you:

a. Show your disappointment!
b. Immediately start asking her what happened – and go over what she had revised.
c. Give her a hug, and console her.
d. Ask her how she feels about it, and respond accordingly.

You want your child to succeed, and that's amazing – but just put yourself in your child's shoes. Imagine you tried hard, did your best, but it just wasn't your day – and then you go home and dread dealing with your mum and dad. You know there will be an inquisition, or even punishment – and it wasn't even your fault. How connected or accepted would you feel? What would this do for your sense of personal power? Even most well-meaning parents can inadvertently damage their child's confidence – by pushing too hard or by being critical. There's another way to motivate your child to do better, and that is acknowledgement! So what is acknowledgement?

Acknowledgement is the act of giving someone productive feedback on what you notice.

Productive feedback can be about anything, whether it's been done well, or needs improvement. People sometimes have an objection with acknowledgement because they feel that it makes the other person arrogant, or "big headed" because we keep praising them. However, you will notice that this definition is not just about "positive" but "productive" feedback. What makes feedback productive is how the person is left feeling afterwards. One can offer feedback about something that needs work, but it's how the feedback is offered that makes the difference. You will know if you have given your child productive feedback when he or she is left feeling connected with you *and* empowered to act. Use the technique I call the **Feedback Sandwich Method** to offer productive feedback. To give this tool a go, take the following steps.

1. Notice something that the child has done well.
2. Talk about what the child could do **even better** next time.
3. Finish with another thing you notice that the child did well.

Think of the example we discussed earlier. You want your child to work harder and improve her grades, so reflect on how you would give feedback here. Do some preparation before launching into the feedback. Make notes of what you noticed your child doing. When did she study? How much time did she spend?

1. Give her feedback about how she studied. Be specific, and state facts (not opinion), for example:
   - I saw that you studied an hour for the test.
   - I saw your notes – they were detailed and tidy.

2. Then talk about how she could improve her test study strategies to make them *even better*. Come up with a specific suggestion rather than an unfocused lecture on how she "should" study more.

   For example:
   - What could make the learning even easier is if you put the phone away while studying.
   - Notes might be even better with mind-mapping.
   - What makes learning even easier if you take breaks for five mins after every forty-five minutes.

3. End with one more specific fact of what she did well.

   For example:
   - You got an A on your last quiz – keep up the good work.
   - I noticed that you are doing homework and turning it in on time.
   - You are going to your teachers for help – asking for help when you need it is a smart strategy.

This allows both parent and child to notice some of the child's achievements. This encourages the child to continue doing even better in the future. It also sends a very positive message to your child that you notice and value them. In addition, this also helps with the child's need for personal power as he or she experiences being capable, self-disciplined, etc. Give this technique a go, especially with repeated behaviours, and make a note of what differences you notice over time.

3. Tools to build positive power

Give A Specific Choice

There are lots of instances when we can give our children choices. The key to success is to offer specific choices. If you are open-ended or vague, but you don't mean to be, this will still send a confusing message to the child. Let's take this example. Your child is back home from school, and it's time for an afternoon snack. You would prefer that your child ate something healthy and had a cup of milk. But since you're trying to give a choice, you ask him:

Parent: "What do you want for a snack?"

Child: "I want French fries."

Parent: "But French Fries aren't healthy, and you had some yesterday."

Child: "But you asked me what I wanted – and I want French fries."

Parent: "You can't have French fries, they aren't good. Have a piece of fruit instead."

How do you think the child would respond to that last statement? The child felt that he was being given a choice, only for it to be taken away. The best way to offer a choice to a child, is to be *specific*, and offer options that you *are happy with*. For example:

- Would you like to have milk or juice with your food?
- Would you like to play outside or inside?
- Would you like to have a banana or an apple?

Take some time out of your day and reflect on some of the daily struggles that you face with your children. Consider which of these situations could be ones where your children could be offered a choice. Take some time to note down possible choices and options that you can offer. This way you are prepared and are not having to make something up in the moment. Preparation will ensure that you are offering choices that you are happy with – and when your children get to choose, they feel empowered as well.

Be very clear with instructions

Have you ever had a disagreement with someone where you felt confused, and just didn't know what the person was on about? Being confused and surprised can be very discouraging for child and adult alike. Imagine what it was like for you when you didn't know why your spouse, parent or sibling was upset? Imagine what it's like for your child to not even know why you're upset, but to be experiencing your upset through yelling or finger pointing. It can be very scary, especially for a younger child.

A common reason why this happens between parents and children is that the child may not have understood what the parent was asking for in the first place. This is because the parent gives their children "negative" instructions. A negative instruction is telling the child what "not" to do, instead of being clear about what you want him or her to do instead. This is done unconsciously, and automatically – so it's not that we are trying to trip our children up. However, we can raise our awareness and understand how this behaviour impacts our kids. Try this little exercise out.

Exercise 5.2: Understanding The Impact Of Negative Instructions

Outcome: To understand what it feels like for your child to hear negative instructions.

Method: You and another adult (your spouse or friend) will do a role play. One of you will be the parent, and the other will be the child. The parent will give the following instructions and the child will carry them through. Be quick with the instructions and the actions, go through the list quickly. Then switch roles and repeat.

1. "Don't look at me."
2. "Don't move around."
3. "Don't stand still."
4. "Don't sit down."
5. "Open your mouth."
6. "Raise your arms above your head."
7. "Stand still."
8. "Lift your left leg up and put it down."

Feedback

Once both of you have done the exercise, exchange notes on how the instructions felt. What was it like to hear the "don't" statements versus the clear instructions about what to do? Which category was easier to follow and why?

Our minds first negate any "don't" statements to do what is being asked. In other words, the mind imagines the action, then negates it. So when parents give children a "don't" statement, the first response is confusion while the child is trying to figure out what is actually expected. When a parent yells, "don't spill the milk" often they will see that the child has spilt the milk. This is not because the child is trying to be defiant, it's just how the brain works. The way to avoid this is to practise giving clear, specific instructions for the behaviour you want. Think about five instructions that you give your child on a regular basis. Reflect on which ones are usually stated as "don't" statements. Come up with the alternative "positive" instruction and write it down. Now you have five, clear, positive instructions to give your child. Put the list up on the fridge or somewhere where you and your child can see them on a regular basis.

This instruction manual will help your child be clear about what's expected, and he or she is much more likely to fulfil expectations when asked. He or she will feel more capable and more in control, and you will also feel more connected and able to communicate better with your child.

Give your child the opportunity to do things himself

Does your child have assigned tasks in the home? Does your child do things that he is capable of? If you have young children, you will notice how they love doing little things alongside you. They love to feel that connection with you and, as they learn things, they get to know that they can do it too. One great way of doing this is to get the family together so everyone has a say. Here's an exercise for the family to do together.

Exercise 5.3: Choosing Family Contributions

Outcome: To help all family members be part of the team and contribute to the daily functioning of the family.

Method: Follow the steps as laid out.

Step 1. Call a family meeting – choose a time when you all can make time to have a fun conversation together.

Step 2. Take turns to say which tasks need to happen to keep the family running. Allow the children to share their ideas. Each person gets a turn. If some of the children are too young to contribute, allow them to sit in – just being there will allow them to be part of the family. One person writes all suggestions down.
Parent: "Let's all take a turn, and say one thing that we need to do regularly to keep our home running well."
Children (in turns):

- Groceries
- Weekly evening out

- Driving us to school
- Tidying up

Step 3. Now figure out how each child will get a turn. Each child will get to pick one or two tasks that they choose to carry out for the month. Give them a choice according to their age. Some tasks will be reserved, specifically for the older children, and some for the younger ones. Use the chart to document the results.

Step 4. The parents will map out their tasks specifically as well. The chart may look something like this.

Table 5.1: Task allocation for family members

Month January 2020	Mom	Dad	Uzair	Rabiah
Pick and drop from school	x			
Paying utility bills		x		
Laying the table				x
Washing up			x	
Folding laundry				x

Put the chart up where the entire family can see it. This way everyone is reminded of what needs to be done. You can also all agree to have a space where tasks on the list are daily marked as "done". Choose whatever strategies empower you to create a family contribution system.

Step 5. At the end of the month, have another meeting. Give each child an opportunity to share what it was like to make their own family contributions. Assignments for the next month could remain the same, or the family can come up with a rotation system, so that the children can do different tasks in the following month.

But I have help so my kids don't need to do anything

Do you have other family members or hired help at home? In many households both parents work full-time, so they have some help with the children as a necessity. However, some parents don't allow their kids to do anything, just because help is available. It's great if you're able to have help, but what impact does it have on your children long term? How will they learn skills that are essential for adult life? Having everything done for them has a disempowering effect on children in the long run. Pampering children in this way sends two very strong subconscious messages:

- There will always be someone there to do things for them.
- They aren't capable of doing things for themselves.

What happens when someone is not available to take care of them? What if they must fend for themselves, how stressful would it be to then have to figure things out? Everything from basic home tasks to managing money can become extremely daunting for young adults if they have not acquired any of these life skills before.

How do working parents with home help find a balanced approach in this situation? Perhaps you can reserve certain tasks that your family does together or individually as well. For example, even if you have help, the children can still make their own beds, or pack their own school lunches. Perhaps you can do certain chores around the house together over the weekend.

Avoid rewards and punishments – make clear rules instead

Do you offer your child rewards for good behaviour? Maybe you give her more technology time for good behaviour, or a pizza for every A? And what do you do when your child misbehaves? You punish her instead? This technique makes a lot of sense on many levels. As a Muslim, you have learnt about reward and punishment from an early age – we all focus on gaining as many rewards from good deeds as possible.

However, I invite you to set this concept aside for a moment. Consider your child as someone who is still learning how to navigate life and is yet to learn how to set his or her expectations about other people and life in general. If we train our children to expect a material reward from another person for every little thing – their expectation of reward will only grow. So let's look at some of the unconscious messages that a child will pick up with this technique of reward and punishment.

1. As a parent, you want the child to learn a good behaviour for its own sake, but the reward strategy does the opposite. The reward is something the child wants, so he carries out the behaviour just for the reward. If the reward stops, so does the behaviour.
2. The child also begins to expect rewards for every good thing he or she does – the list can become endless.
3. The current reward being offered will lose its allure, so you will be forced to dangle a bigger carrot to get the same result.
4. When a reward is withheld as part of a punishment, it only leaves the child feeling angry and disconnected from the parent. The Oxford College Dictionary defines punishment as "the infliction or imposition of a penalty as a retribution for an offense". Inflicting pain on anyone doesn't make them think about what they did, it keeps them focused on the pain. Pain, anger, or stress engages the fight–flight mechanism. The state of fight–flight stops us from engaging the parts of the brain that consider consequences. The bottom line is that you will not get the desired result because your child will not absorb the lesson you wish to teach.

Use clear rules and consequences instead

Imagine if you were given a reward at work, and it was then taken away because you did something that the boss didn't like. How would that feel? Punishments of this sort result in feelings of humiliation and disconnection. Rules work differently. When a regulation is laid out at work, employees either comply or deal with the consequences that have already been laid out. An adult has the choice to comply with a rule or not, but knows too that non-compliance has consequences. For example, there are several employers who have a timesheet policy. If employees arrive late, leave early, or are absent, then the consequences are followed through automatically.

In the same way, when clear rules are set out, children know what they're supposed to do. They also have a clear idea of the **consequences** when they don't do what's expected. However, if this were a reward-based strategy, then the child knows the behaviour is desired, not expected. If the child wants the reward, he will do that thing, but if the reward no longer motivates him, he will just stop doing it. On the other hand, rules teach the child that actions have consequences, which builds self-discipline in the long run. Let's explore how to set clear rules.

Exercise 5.4: Setting Clear Rules And Consequences

Outcome: To support parents to set clear rules for their children, so that discipline is maintained and tantrums are reduced.

Method: Answer the questions and follow the steps accordingly.

Step 1: Clarification
Make a list of the misbehaviours that occur repeatedly in your home. For example:

- Not making the bed.
- Forgetting to do homework.
- Leaving dirty dishes in the sink.

Step 2: Creating Rules
Take your time in carrying out the following steps, as the more prepared you are, the better the results will be.

1. Think about the top five issues (if you have less, that's great), and reflect on specific rules that you want to create for each of these. Aim to resolve the biggest issues, and work on those first. Refrain from long lists. If you have multiple children in the home,

reflect on the biggest issues that are common for all of them, and choose those. Avoid setting different rules for individual children as this can cause feelings of disconnection and rivalry.

2. Come up with very specific, and easy to understand rules. For example:

- Making the bed before coming down for breakfast.
- Homework is to be written down by due date, and completed before dinner time.
- Wash your breakfast dishes before leaving for school.

Step 3: Creating the consequence
This may be the most difficult part of this exercise because it requires both thoughtfulness and willingness to follow through. Keep the following things in mind:

1. The consequence **must** be related to the behaviour. Avoid using unrelated punishments such as "grounding" or "no TV" as they will not make sense to the child, and just feel unreasonable causing your child to feel humiliated or angry.
2. You *must* be willing to follow through on the consequence. If you're feeling even slightly hesitant, then choose a different consequence.
3. Once the rule is broken, act on the consequence. Avoid explaining and rationalizing why you are following through.

Step 4: Display the rules and talk them through
Next, write out the rules with the consequences for rule-breaking so they are visible to everyone in the family. The rules apply to all the members of the household. If a rule is broken, the stated consequences follow. The chart can look something like this:

Table 5.2: Establishing rules with consequences

Rule	Consequence when broken
Make your bed before breakfast.	If you forget to make your bed, you will come home from school and make it. You will make one of your sibling's bed the next day (can name the sibling).
Homework should be completed before dinner.	If homework remains incomplete. No relaxation time. Homework to be finished before bedtime.
Your breakfast dishes to be washed before leaving for school.	If you leave dishes in the sink, you will wash everyone's dinner dishes that night.

A few points to keep in mind:

- Be clear if the rules apply to the kids, or to everyone! (If they apply to everyone, then you will be subject to the same consequences.)
- Just lay out the rules as matters of fact. They are not up for debate or discussion.
- Ensure that all adults in the family are willing to follow through. If not, this can create a very challenging family dynamic. Have this discussion before presenting the rules to the kids.
- When a rule is broken, take calm and clear action. Avoid explaining and rationalizing.

In the beginning, it will be difficult for all of you to adjust to the new system. However, in time, everyone will become accustomed to clear rules and boundaries. Once the consequences have been felt a few times, the children will start gaining a sense of personal accountability and power. And they will be learning important life skills as well.

Our work together has been focused on understanding that children's behaviour is driven by their need to feel valued and be seen as capable members of the family. Give the suggested tools a go and adapt them as you need to. Go ahead, be flexible, and enjoy the process. Here are a few more general strategies to keep in mind.

1. It's okay for you to take a time out

One of the most effective strategies to help a child throwing a tantrum to calm down is to send him to take a "time out" in his room. Time outs are a great strategy to use – they help the child calm down and break the tantrum or diffuse feelings of anger. Parents can also lose their cool from time to time. If you find that you're about to lose your cool, take a time out yourself. It's okay to take a break before reacting. Just say something like "I'm very upset with you right now. I need to take a few minutes to calm down, and we will talk about this when I come back." Then go into your room, take a few deep breaths and come back when you're ready.

2. Comment on the behaviour, not the child

Let's face it, children can test even the most patient of parents. The most well-meaning parent can end up using bad language or criticizing their child in the heat of the moment. In addition, if we aren't aware, we may be inadvertently criticizing the child, when we only want to comment on their behaviour. See if you can recognize any of the following statements:

- "What's wrong with you? Are you crazy? What were you thinking?"
- "Bad girl, how many times have I told you not to touch that?"
- "I can't believe you're my child. I'm so disappointed in you!"

Do any of the above sound familiar? Have you ever said them, or maybe they were said to you? How do you think they would impact your child? Statements of this nature can truly wound children. You may have been angry, but instead of commenting on the behaviour, you made a comment about your child's character. This sends the message that they are not good enough. How might this impact their need for feeling valued? It's okay to express anger at your child's behaviour, but keep it specific to the behaviour. Avoid talking about their character. For example:

- Please keep away from that. It will get damaged if it's touched this way.
- I love you and you're a good daughter, but I feel disappointed with what you did.
- Can you please tell me what you were thinking about when you decided to do this?

Think back to when you may have commented on your child's character. Think of alternate statements you could make instead. This effort will prepare you for any situation that may come up in the future.

3. Apologize when you yell or say something inappropriate

Parents are human too! It's important to apologize if you get upset or say something inappropriate. Children are very forgiving, so your effort to apologize will help to repair any distance. Your children will also learn how to ask for forgiveness. You will be modelling what they need to learn.

4. Say please and thank you

If you want a well-mannered child, then you need to model good manners. When you say please and thank you, your child's confidence goes up because he feels respected and valued. He also learns good manners!

5. Do something different!

If you discover that your current strategies are not working, then go ahead and try something different. Parenting requires learning and skill-building as well. So be brave and try something new. In the beginning, even your child may notice and be surprised, but you won't know if a strategy is good until you've tried it out.

Let's summarise the main points

- We talked about parenting style.
- We talked about children's need for positive power and connection.
- We explored how certain behaviours from parents may disempower children.
- We explored tools that can be used to build positive power.
- We explored tools that can be used to build connection between the child and the parent.
- We explored a few different general strategies to keep in mind.

6.

Cultivating Fulfilment in Your Marriage

Another of His signs is that He created spouses from among yourselves for you to live with in tranquillity: He ordained love and kindness between you.

Qur'an 30:21

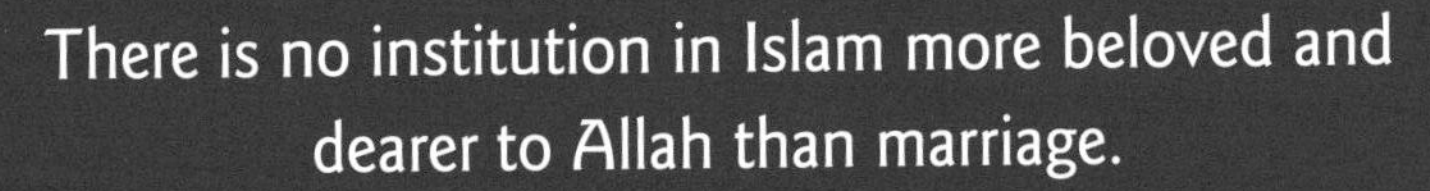

There is no institution in Islam more beloved and dearer to Allah than marriage.

Prophet Muhammad (pbuh)

Married people and single people share something in common

Are you looking for "the one"? Perhaps you aren't ready yet, but you're experiencing a lot of family pressure to get married. Maybe you're already married, but are having some issues within your marriage. Whatever your circumstance, it's probably safe to say that you want to change your current situation in some way. Despite the obvious differences, there is one important thing that single and married people have in common. Both these groups hold assumptions and expectations regarding marriage. We all hold assumptions about various aspects of our lives. Assumptions help us make sense of human experience. So what is an assumption?

An assumption is an unexamined thought that we commonly take to be true.

People make assumptions all the time. We accept some as common "truths" about life without really exploring their validity. We form others from our own experience, what we hear and see growing up, and what our caregivers tell us. Let's understand this further by noting some commonly held assumptions.

- Things will work out.
- Certain things are just plain common sense.
- Hard work is essential to succeed.

If you analyse any of the above statements, you will notice that they are not based on specific facts. They are just beliefs many of us commonly hold to be true. Please note that this behaviour is just part of our human makeup. We automatically assume things all the time. Our assumptions vary because they do emerge from our own unique experiences, but we also find that many are common and accepted as widely-held "truths." Since we make assumptions in all areas of our lives, this also means that we make assumptions about being married as well. Let's look at some of the more common ones.

Common assumptions about marriage

- My spouse should/will be someone who completes me.
- My spouse should be my best friend.
- We will live happily ever after.
- S/he will change after marriage – it will be okay!

Which of these statements do you believe are true? Which ones sound familiar? There are any number of assumptions, but these are the ones I've heard many times before. Our assumptions, though automatic and ongoing, impact us greatly. We will explore how they do that a little bit later, but first I invite you to take some time to explore your own assumptions. Ask yourself the following:

Choose your top three most important assumptions about marriage.

I think or believe that marriage is, or should be:

1. ______________________________
2. ______________________________
3. ______________________________

Assumptions have an impact

Our assumptions often become enmeshed with or turn into expectations. For example, if you assume that "family should be there for one another," then you believe that as a truth. This truth will naturally lead to the expectation that *my family will be there for me because family "should" be there for one another*. In this situation, the assumption and expectation are essentially the same. You may not have articulated it, but that doesn't nullify the expectation. Imagine that you are suddenly taken ill, or something bad happens, and some close family members are unable to support you at that time. How would that feel? You would be disappointed, wouldn't you? Have you experienced something like this before? If you have, then you now have a clearer picture of the role that assumptions play in creating our expectations. Let's go one step further and get clarity on what an expectation is.

An expectation is when we predict or bank on a particular outcome or situation to happen.

It now probably makes sense how assumptions and expectations can either be tied together or be one and the same. Now you may be thinking that expectations are bad. But having expectations is a natural human instinct, so please avoid falling into the trap of telling yourself that you shouldn't expect anything; that is an expectation itself! The key is to become aware of your expectations and figure out which ones are realistic and which ones need some tweaking. *Even though assumptions are automatic and perhaps, uncontrollable, expectations can still be tweaked!*

We naturally have expectations from romantic relationships

Let's turn towards marriage now. Human beings, whether married or single (or looking), have one expectation in common. **They enter into a marriage expecting that their spouse will meet their needs!** This is the most fundamental expectation that most people have when they enter a marriage. Yet many of us are not trained to accept, even admit that we hold this expectation. So is it bad to hold this expectation? Not at all, in fact, it's a natural human instinct. It's natural for us to expect that our spouse will meet our needs. That said, it's even more important to answer two questions first:

1. What our individual needs are.
2. Which of our needs we can realistically expect our spouse to fulfil.

Generally, our expectations around romantic, loving relationships start forming when we are young. As we grow up, we are bombarded with opinions from our families, friends and social media. In fact, it's these very opinions, assumptions and expectations that guide our choice for a spouse in the first place. For example, if someone has an expectation that their spouse will be just as religious, or as family oriented as they are, then that will shape their search accordingly.

However, one serious issue that often comes up in marriage is that spouses become disappointed with each other. This happens because their expectations are not being met. But if we look even deeper, what commonly happens is that the spouses aren't aware of each other's expectations at all, so there's no chance of them being met. At times, people don't even know their own expectations. They are hidden from their own view. It might be alright if they stayed that way, but unspoken or undiscovered expectations have a way of showing up. Have you ever found yourself in a situation where you're feeling angry and resentful? You're not sure why it's happening, but you can't seem to shake it. This is what classically happens when unspoken expectations aren't fulfilled.

In many Muslim families, even the thought of speaking about expectations is considered selfish. In particular, girls are taught that they will need to compromise and put their husbands' needs above their own. They may succeed in doing this for some time, but there's no telling when the resentment, anger or anxiety may surface.

Case Study: Umayma

I was approached by a mother who said that her teenage daughter Umayma was having issues with her husband. She brought her daughter to meet with me. The parents had gotten Umayma engaged at fourteen, apparently with her permission. Umayma was now 16, her Islamic marriage (nikah) having been performed a few months earlier. Umayma was panicking about the impending wedding, which is to take place in a year. The groom felt that Umayma didn't like him, and wanted to call the whole thing off. Umayma's mother brought her daughter to me, fearing she would let a perfectly good match go and then be labelled as a "divorcee". She wanted me to counsel Umayma out of her anxiety. As I sat with Umayma, who was clearly upset and anxious, I asked her about what she was afraid of. She was very hesitant to share anything with me. However, when I asked her to tell me her thoughts on marriage, what marriage meant to her, she only said one word, "Compromise."

I thought it was essential to talk with Umayma's mum who admitted she raised all her daughters with the expectation that marriage is compromise. She had not talked to her girls about the rights of women, nor had she spoken of companionship or love. When I asked Umayma's mum if she had been taught about any of the good aspects of marriage, she admitted she had not. So I coached the mother and explained that if someone is taught to expect only compromise and restriction, then it's no wonder that Umayma felt anxious and upset about her marriage. If she was stepping into a future where she could expect to only compromise and give in, why not talk to her about her own needs? She probably has some hopes and dreams of her own, so why would she be happy to step into a life of compromise? She promised to talk to Umayma about the positive aspects about marriage, and give her daughter the space to speak about her feelings and take some of the time pressure off Umayma with the impending marriage.

We will all have some expectations. If anyone tells you that they don't expect anything – please give them some encouragement and space to explore this. They may be unaware, or perhaps afraid to express their expectations out of fear of rejection. So how do we explore our expectations?

Exercise 6.1: Exploring Expectations

Outcome: To raise your awareness of your expectations.

Method: You begin by writing down your assumptions from the previous little exercise, and then follow the table from there: Follow the table headings below and fill the columns in.

Table 6.1: Exploring assumptions and expectations regarding marriage

My top 3–5 beliefs/ assumptions about marriage are:	Looking at my assumptions, I think that my top 3–5 expectations are:	Which of these expectations have I communicated to my spouse or prospective spouse?
(e.g.) Marriage is being with my best friend.	(e.g.) I expect him to be there when I need to talk.	
1.	1.	1.
2.	2.	2.
3.	3.	3.
4.	4.	4.
5.	5.	5.

Feedback

Now that you have a raised awareness of what your expectations are, it might be useful to deepen this awareness further. The following questions are designed to help you notice how well you've been communicating your expectations up to the present moment:

1. Did I know I had these expectations? (yes/no)
2. What expectations have now become apparent, which I didn't even know I had?
3. On a scale of 1–10, 10 being extremely clearly, how clearly have I voiced my expectations to my spouse/ prospective spouse?

1	2	3	4	5	6	7	8	9	10

Unclear and not explained — Clear and understood

4. What efforts have I made to clearly understand my spouse's expectations?

5. On a scale of 1–10, how often have I met expectations in a way that s/he feels fulfilled?

1	2	3	4	5	6	7	8	9	10

Hardly ever (I always get it wrong) — All the time!

6. What is first thing that I am going to do differently now?

We all keep score!

What did you learn from the previous exercise? How clearly have you communicated your expectations to your spouse? I can imagine that you have some new insights. Also note that our expectations have a way of revealing themselves even when we aren't addressing them. They show up through unresolved issues. For example, have you ever been caught in an argument where your spouse brought up something from the past? Perhaps it was something that you said or did that hurt them? Did this comment catch you completely off-guard? You thought the incident was over and resolved a long time ago – and then you find yourselves having the same old argument all over again. Does this sound familiar? If so, you are really not alone.

So why is it that old hurts and resentments keep rearing their ugly heads? Is it you who remembers old wounds, or is it your spouse? Usually one person remembers the issues, and then the other person also chimes in with their own hurts. Consider that **old resentments continue to show up because the root cause hasn't been handled yet!** Each time our spouse's expectation is not met, it will bring up all the other times the same thing happened. It may seem like a new issue, but deep down the same root cause has not been handled. You see, most people aren't good at just letting expectations go; this is because they are just part of natural human wants. What we do instead is keep track of when our expectations were met or not. My father gave me some wonderful advice years ago, he said that, "Marriage is like a bank account: you get back what you put in." I would now like to add to this, it's not only marriage, instead:

Our unconscious mind creates a debit–credit account for every meaningful relationship we forge. We do this naturally and unconsciously. We will call this unconscious account the "Relationship Reserve".

We create a Relationship Reserve automatically and unconsciously for all meaningful relationships. Each relationship has its own ledger. When the person lives up to an expectation, they get positive credits, and when they disappoint, they get debited from our own unconscious account. Remember that as you are doing this, others have an account for you too – this includes your spouse! This behaviour isn't evil or selfish. It's natural human behaviour to have expectations; this is how we identify whether we are happy in a situation or not. Remember, the other people in your life are human too so they will be doing the same thing unconsciously. The expectations differ, but the scoring behaviour is natural and human. This concept is being brought up just to raise your awareness to it. There are, of course, many other behaviours such as consciously offering forgiveness and love that can elevate us above keeping score.

Coming back to marriage, think about how you gauge your fulfilment in your marriage. Fill in the blanks to the following statements to raise your awareness around how you're scoring your spouse at present.

Awareness exercise: My spouse's relationship score:

Method: Complete the sentences below:

I'm fulfilled in this relationship because ______________________

____

My spouse meets my need for ______________________________

______________________ ______________________

I know that my spouse meets these needs because I see (him/her)
doing ______________________________ for me/ with me
saying ______________________________ to me/ about me
being ______________________________________

My spouse is currently not meeting my need for______________

I think this might be because ______________________________
I don't see, hear, experience my spouse doing or saying

____

My spouse's Relationship Reserve score is ____________________
(give them a score from 1–10).

1 2 3 4 5 6 7 8 9 10

I think my score within (your spouse's name)'s Relationship Reserve might be ________________. I am assuming this because:

____

Tip: You may ask your spouse to score you as well. However, only do this if you are both ready to work on the relationship together. This process may make things more difficult, so if you are even a little bit hesitant, then avoid this at present. Keep in mind that you may find the information surprising (and possibly not as positive as you may expect). Please remember to only ask for feedback if you can be receptive without a reaction. If not, this can only cause more issues.

My expectations are low – so why am I disappointed?

Are you someone who keeps their expectations low? You remind yourself not to "expect much" from certain people, yet you find that you feel disappointed and hurt from time to time, and maybe you can't figure out why? This is because your unconscious mind is still keeping score – as it always does. So you are unconsciously debiting points from the relationship without even realizing it. You seem to keep your expectations low, and you even psyche yourself up to be prepared for disappointment, and then it happens! This is because your brain has been using past experiences to predict what will happen next time; to prepare you to deal with it. Consider that somewhere, there are expectations that have not been voiced, but are still needing to be met. The most productive thing to do at this time is to first admit to yourself that there may be some unmet expectations and that you are unconsciously keeping score. This person's account in your Relationship Reserve is either low or may even be overdrawn.

Start to notice the scores with specific relationships and begin to then explore why the scores are low, manageable or high within these relationships. Start playing around with the above questions, and soon you will get an idea of how we naturally keep score all the time; we just aren't aware that we do. Please remember that even though we score people in this way, our values around maintaining relationships can win the day. This is how we can transform relationships that may not be working – just by transforming our own thoughts and behaviours in that relationship. Also keep in mind that you can only raise your own awareness and work on your own thoughts and behaviours. The good news is, that one person's shift can impact the relationship for both people in a productive way.

Expectations are a blanket for needs

Before we explore this further, let's connect the dots. Human beings always assume and expect things – we do this pretty much all the time! Of course, each human being does so, depending on his or her specific circumstances. We create a picture of how things should be, we become attached to certain outcomes, and do all this because we are trying to get our needs met!

Upon reflection, you will note that expectations are really a blanket that covers up our basic needs. Expectations are an indirect way of expressing our needs. For example, a person might feel too vulnerable to say, "I need love and attention." It's somehow easier to say something like "My loved ones/my family should be there for me." Stating our needs in this way does serves a couple of purposes, but it also has some disadvantages, so let's take a look:

Table 6.2: Exploring advantages and disadvantages of stating my needs

Advantages of stating my needs as expectations	Disadvantages of stating my needs as expectations
I am less vulnerable, so the fear of someone rejecting me or my needs is reduced.	The other person doesn't see my vulnerability, which is a lost opportunity to connect. In fact, they may perceive me as selfish or unyielding.
I place responsibility on the other person to fulfil my needs.	I am disappointed when my need is not met.
I get to believe that the desired outcome can come true. It's a need that can be met.	There is no guarantee that the other person will understand my need, or even necessarily be able to meet it.
As a Muslim, I have certain rights that I can expect. My faith has given me permission to respectfully discuss them, even if I've not seen it done in my family and community.	The actual need that I'm trying to meet may become clouded in conversations about expectations. I/we need to have honest, vulnerable communication in my marriage (and other relationships).

Creating expectations is one behaviour through which we are trying to communicate our needs. As we know, **expectations arise when we become attached to a certain outcome: our focus is on the outcome, rather than expressing the deeper need underneath**. The outcome is the specific behaviour that's desired. However, the actual need may be fulfilled through some other behaviour as well.

For example, when someone is expecting that their loved ones "will be there", the outcome they may expect is the person's physical presence. However, the need underneath might be love, support or affirmation. That love and support could be provided in other ways, such as making a phone call, sending a care package, or just being a shoulder to cry on. But if the person is attached to the "outcome" they may debit the relationship reserve if the person couldn't be physically present (though their support may well have been there). This is a very important point to understand because at times we may be attached to the outcome, while ignoring the real need underneath. Just keep in mind that it is the need that is most important, and the desired outcome can be shifted. Take this opportunity to list your own expectations to explore the real need underneath them.

Exercise 6.2: Exploring The Need Underneath The Expectation

Method: Write down your expectations from the above exercise and fill in the rest of the table.

Table 6.3: Exploring what I really need

My expectation from my spouse is that ________	**What do I really need? (Affection, conversation, undivided attention, etc.)**	**How does having this need met make me feel? (Loved, important, connected, beautiful, etc.)**
We will do home projects together.	Support	Loved, respected
We will discuss each of our activities at the end of the day.	Attention, conversation	Connected, loved

Feedback:

1. What are my most important needs? List them as single words such as: support, conversation, attention, connection, affection etc.

2. Does my spouse know that I have these needs? If I ask my spouse, what would he or she say?
3. Does my spouse know what behaviours help me meet this need? For example, does he know that hugs and affection make me feel that I'm loved?
4. How might I communicate my needs to him more effectively?

Tip: if you want to further improve your marriage, I invite you to ask your spouse to also do this exercise – that way you get to know his or her needs more clearly as well!

Complaints are another way of expressing an unfulfilled need

Isn't it interesting how our expectations are about having our needs met? Many people don't express their expectations or their needs directly – they use stories instead. Have you ever come across someone who has a story about what their spouse has done wrong? Each time you speak, they have a "new" complaint about how they were let down. If they were to look at their stories more objectively, they would notice that the stories have a pattern.

Storytelling is another way we express our anger, resentment and unfulfilled needs. This type of negative storytelling has two issues. The first is that there's no end to the story; each time an event happens, we just add to the story, even though the essential issue remains the same. The second concern is that we can get so wrapped up and lost in the story, that we even lose touch with the real disappointment that lies underneath. Remember that the story is all about an unfulfilled need or want, and the only way to release it and move on is to get to the heart of the matter and deal with it. Have you been caught up in a story about your relationship? Keep in mind that if you continue to be so, it can have a devastating impact on your marriage in the long term. So if you're feeling caught up in all the events of the past, take some time to work with the following exercise. *Insha'Allah*, you will be able to get to the real issues by exploring your unmet needs.

Exercise 6.3: Identifying The Main Complaint Underneath The Story

Outcome: To explore what the deeper issue in the relationship is.

Method: Answer the questions as you go along.

Part 1: The Story
Answer these questions in your coaching journal.

1. Write a story of what it's like being married to your spouse. Write down the good things, as well as your complaints. Notice what's getting to you, notice which subjects lead to the same arguments again and again. Take a page or two to do this. Then answer the other questions.

2. Take a moment to make a table like this and fill it out to the best of your ability:

Table 6.4: Exploring my Relationship Reserve

Relationship Reserve Debits	Relationship Reserve Credits
List down the behaviours that take away the most points. Also write down how many debits each behaviour has (you get to choose this).	List down your spouse's behaviours that add the most credit to his score. Also write down how many credits each behaviour gets:
Leaving things untidy (2)	Bringing me gifts (5)
Not calling when he'll be late (5)	Spending time with my parents without being asked (5)
Being on the phone at dinner time (10)	Making breakfast on Sunday (3)

1. On a scale of 1–10, my spouse's score in my Relationship Reserve is

1	2	3	4	5	6	7	8	9	10

Very low/depleted very high (I feel fulfilled)

2. I am giving him/her this score because what I see, hear, feel and experience is ________________

Feedback

What did you learn from the previous section? Is the Relationship Reserve score low, or do you now find that your spouse does a lot of things to meet your needs? If you find that your debits far exceed your credits, then the chances are that some important needs are not being met. If so, then proceed to the next section.

Part 2: Identifying unmet needs:

Look at the table above, and notice which behaviours are creating debits in the reserve. Then ask yourself the following.

My biggest complaint/s with my spouse is/are ____________________

Note: just list down a few main complaints from your story – avoid making a long list!

a.

b.

c.

- Why does this behaviour bother me?
- How do I feel when my spouse does this?
- The impact of my feelings on our relationship is that I

____

- What do I really need my spouse, to do instead?

____

- And when my spouse does this, I feel ___________________
- So what I really need from my spouse is_______________ (use the behaviour and the feeling, to explore the real need, for example, attention, affection, connection, etc.)

- When I don't have this need met, I feel

____

- When this need is met, it allows me to

____

Part 3: Communicating the need

1. Does this need show up as a need when I am nagging / complaining about / arguing with my spouse about his or her behaviour?
2. Does my spouse even know what my real need is?
3. How have I tried to communicate my needs in the past?
4. On a scale of 1–10, how effective has my communication been?

1	2	3	4	5	6	7	8	9	10

(not at all/ they didn't get it) (spot on, it's been dealt with)

5. How might I communicate my needs differently now?

What did you learn from this exercise? I hope that you noticed some credits in your Relationship Reserve account, maybe you noticed that your spouse has more in the reserve than you previously thought. All this counting may well seem petty, but the hard truth is that we keep score whether we like to admit it or not. I can't imagine anyone readily admitting that they keep score because human beings do this at an unconscious level. Frankly, it is not a bad thing because it helps us to identify those relationships that nurture us verses those that don't. In fact, this "score keeping" takes place at a very obvious level in some cultures. For example, in some cultures, every gift received at a wedding or birthday is written down and reciprocated with a gift of an equal or greater value when the other party has an occasion. In this way, both parties feel appreciated and acknowledged.

Do all your needs require your spouse?

All the self-reflection in this chapter has been geared towards figuring out what you need from your spouse, and whether he or she understands what it is that you truly need. **But is it your spouse's responsibility to meet all your needs?** Your first instinct might have been a resounding yes, but let's look at this in a bit more depth.

- Do you believe that you meet all of your spouse's needs?
- Or are there any needs that you believe you can't meet? What might those needs be?

If you feel you can't meet all your spouse's needs, then be sure that your spouse feels the same way! He or she also has limited resources , and so having an expectation that your spouse will fulfil all your needs is unrealistic.

Exercise 6.4: Division Of Needs

Outcome: To explore who can meet specific needs that you have.

Method: This exercise may take time, so work through the table at your own pace. Use the example if it helps.

Table 6.5: Exploring how I can have my needs met

What is my need	Can I meet this need myself? If so, how?	If I cannot meet this need, who can? How can he/she meet this need? (List down all possible sources – human and otherwise)	Is this need being met at this time?
To share my activities and achievements. This gives me connection.	No. I need to talk to someone else; my need is to share and connect. Thinking about it, I could write in my diary or planner, when I don't have someone to talk to. That would help make things clearer.	My spouse can meet it Friends can meet it (mention specific friends if appropriate)	Yes, but not all the time. I sometimes want to talk and no one is available.

What does this simple exercise open up for you? It's essential that we don't put all our needs into one single basket. Once we begin to separate out our needs, we can manage our expectations and our relationships more effectively. It may also be that certain needs are met through more than one source. For example, many women have a strong need for affection. This need may be met by more than their spouse. Although affection from a spouse is special, and still required, some of the need can be fulfilled through hugs from children. You will find that most people will have the same needs as you, but your way of meeting your needs will differ from others. The greater clarity you have on what you need from where, the better your chances of success. If you think of your needs as goals that need to be met, then it all makes sense, doesn't it?

Breaking disempowering patterns

The biggest difference between a need and any other goal is that a need sits like a mandatory requirement whereas a goal may or may not be achieved. Someone I know says it the best: there are those things that we "need" and then there are others that are "nice to have". For example, the need for money is a necessity to live, but after you have what you need, additional money is often used to provide enjoyment or security. Needs are in the driving seat: this goes for all types of needs, whether physical, emotional or spiritual. In other words, we can't really feel fulfilled or content until the need is met. It's an unconscious drive that gears us towards meeting our needs.

Now let's focus back to marriage. Many marriages run into trouble when relationship needs aren't being met on a regular basis. Any type of interaction that is happening regularly is a pattern. So if we have certain behaviours that meet our needs, these are empowering patterns, and ones that don't are disempowering. If you argue a lot over the same things, consider that you both have fallen into a pattern that doesn't work. Issues may become further exacerbated if needs are not being met over a long period of time. The person whose needs aren't being met looks outside the relationship or leaves it altogether. I know this makes it sound like most people are selfish, but aren't we, if we are truly honest about it? Would people stay in marriages where their own needs aren't met? They may stay, but the resentment, hurt or anger will creep in. It's natural.

So are you considering ending your marriage because your needs aren't being met? Are you feeling resentful or angry at present? Such emotions can override our ability to calculate consequences, and we may end up doing something that we later regret. If you are feeling emotionally charged, then find ways to regain your sense of calm before you make any big decisions. In the meantime, even though you may be feeling resentful, and your spouse's account is running on a deficit, I invite you to consider two ideas.

If your needs aren't being met, your spouse's needs aren't being met either.

No matter what your matrimonial reserve is (your spouse's credit with you), focus on meeting your spouse's needs, and let go of focusing on your own for the time being.

The second idea may sound really crazy, especially if you're already feeling resentful or hurt. But remember that relationships don't change on their own. Sure, Allah sends different life and relationship challenges our way to help us grow. These challenges are a sign to help us notice our reactions and behaviours so we can improve and realize our potential. The point to note here is that the way we conduct ourselves through these relationship challenges will stay the same unless we make a conscious effort to change something. So if you are feeling unhappy or resentful, it's very likely that your spouse is feeling the same. Keep these thoughts in mind, and give the short exercise below a go.

Exercise 6.5: Noticing The Future

Outcome: To explore how keeping things the same will impact the future of your marriage.

Method: Answer the questions in your coaching journal.

Step 1: Noticing the issue

Bring one significant issue in your relationship to the fore. Write down the problem.

Step 2: Visualization

Bring the most recent incident to mind. Close your eyes and bring your memory of the event to mind. See yourself and your spouse and watch the event unfolding. You are watching it as if it were a movie and the people in it are characters. You are an observer. Your aim is to notice:

- How the event begins.
- What each person says and does.
- How it proceeds.
- And notice how it ends.
- And notice the impact over the next few hours, or days after the event.

Once your movie has run its course, open your eyes and write down everything you can remember.

Step 3: Noticing the future

Imagine that nothing changes, and this type of incident keeps recurring over the long term. How might this recurring situation impact you, your spouse, and your overall life:
In the next six months? After a year? After five years? *Is this a future you want to live in to?* Are you looking forward to it?

What was your answer to the last question? We can often predict our future by exploring our behaviour in the present. If you answered no to the last couple of questions, then that is a strong indicator that the current pattern needs to be interrupted and broken. Patterns are formed by a repetitive cycle of stimulus and response, so *the only way that we can break a pattern is to do something, one thing, differently!* There is a lot more on this in the chapter on stress, so go ahead and take a look at that. But coming back to our topic, this essentially means that you would need to do something differently; even if you feel that it's a struggle, or you don't want to. But if you keep your eye on creating a better pattern, then it will make your effort worth it.

Let's look at an example to better understand this:

Case Study: Shaheena

Shaheena feels frustrated in her marriage because she is always craving the attention that she feels is lacking from her husband. Her biggest gripe is that he is always on the phone when he is home. When he is not talking to people, he's just surfing the net or answering WhatsApp messages. He's on the phone at the dining table, in the bedroom, so on and so forth. She has tried talking to him about it, gently taking the phone away, requesting him to look at her, but each time she tries anything, they end up in an argument. She feels frustrated and angry – each negative interaction affects them both for days and the stress is affecting their marriage. Her husband has told her that he feels controlled and that gets him even more upset. This negative pattern has become a large part of their everyday life.

After some serious soul searching, Shaheena realized that if she continues her approach, the frustrations in their marriage will continue to build, and neither one of them will get their needs met. She understood that she was trying to get him to do something he was unprepared to do. Her husband's behaviour was meeting a need for him, or was important to him for his own reasons. His need is valid, and her need is valid as well.

Understanding this helped her, because she realized that it doesn't have to be one or the other, but both spouses should have their needs met.

She decided to take on a different approach to break the toxic pattern. She allowed him his time on the phone, especially in the morning, and last thing at night. She also asked him what he really needed; he said that he really needed to keep on top of work e-mails, and clean up all the junk messages he was getting. Staying connected is an important value for him, and she's learning to respect that. The more space she started giving him, the more time he was willing to spend with her. She found that when she really needed to talk, and made a request, he was more willing to give her time. She began carving out a plan that met both their needs; she started focusing on being more available when he was available. But if she hadn't been willing to do so the pattern would have continued.

How do I break the pattern?

Are you ready to break the pattern? For the pattern to break, the most important step is to become aware of one's own contribution to the pattern continuing. Okay, so your spouse hasn't been meeting your needs, but what have you been doing as a reaction to his or her behaviour? Breaking a pattern begins with awareness and personal accountability. So reflect on the following question:

Which of your spouse's needs have you been unwilling to fulfil, as a punishment, due to your own resentments?

This question is quite harsh, and you may feel that it's unfair. However, just take a deep breath and look at the pattern from the above exercise. Just take on the idea that if your spouse seems unyielding or is upsetting you, then you too may have come across as being careless or unwilling to meet a certain need for him or her. It might simply be the need to sleep on time, to be left alone, or have some space. Whatever it is, this pattern is there because there's an unmet need from the other side as well! Imagine that someone asks your spouse on a scale of 1–10 how fulfilled he or she is in their marriage, what number might they give and why?

The first step to breaking the pattern is to focus on your spouse's need, especially one that's important to them. Once you begin to meet this need for your spouse, you will find that your spouse is more fulfilled, and therefore more responsive as well, *insha'Allah*. It may be that you're unclear about what your spouse needs, so now might be a good time to explore this. Work through the questions.

Exercise 6.6: Understanding My Spouse's Needs Better

Outcome: To understand what your spouse really needs, so that you can begin to fulfil it.

Method: Work through the questions below.

Understanding the situation from your spouse's point of view
The previous exercise was about noticing a recurrent, negative pattern between you and your spouse. You had the opportunity to explore how the situation impacts you. Now take a look at it from the other perspective by putting yourself in your spouse's shoes.

You can do this in a creative way. Put two chairs across from each other, not too far away. Label one chair as you, and the other as your spouse. Just imagine that you are shifting chairs, to appreciate a different vantage point for the same situation.

Step 1: Bringing a situation to mind
Stand in a neutral zone between the two chairs. Recall a situation that has been a constant negative pattern in your marriage. I suggest you choose the same one from the previous exercise, but you can choose another. Bring it to mind as clearly as possible, before you proceed. Visualize the event, again from a neutral position for the moment. This is to jog your memory.

Step 2: From your spouse's point of view
Now go and sit on the chair that you labelled as your spouse's. Imagine that you are now your spouse, noticing everything from his or her perspective, therefore you are looking at your own behaviour from your spouse's point of view. You are in his or her shoes now. Start to visualize the event as-if you are your spouse. Step into it as fully as you can. Notice

- Your body language
- Your tone of voice
- Your words
- Your mood

Notice all the details that you can, and when you are ready, stand up and go back to the middle. Give your body a shake. (this is very important!)

Step 3: Seeing the big picture
Stand in the position in the middle, between the two chairs. You are now able to observe what your spouse said, their reactions, and perhaps even their feelings. From this neutral position, it's time to gain awareness of the bigger picture, without taking any sides. You already know how you feel about this situation. You remember what your spouse says and does. Now that you have some awareness of your spouse's experience of your behaviour. So, take this awareness and fill in the following table.

Table 6.6: Exploring different points of view

	From my spouse's point of view: How does my spouse experience me in this situation?	**My own point of view:** How do I feel and experience my spouse in this situation?
Specific words being used		
Body language		
Tone of voice		
Action		
How the interaction ends		

What are you learning about how your spouse experiences your behaviour?

Step 4: Identifying needs and next steps

You may now have more information and insight into what your spouse may be experiencing. This is the opportunity to explore what your spouse needs from you. Once you begin to meet this need, you can break the toxic pattern you both find yourselves in. Answer the following questions in your journal:

1. By evaluating this one, specific pattern, what do I now understand that my spouse needs from me?
2. Am I willing to ask him, to verify that this is what he needs? If not, why? And if yes, then by when shall I do so?

Proceed after you have the answer to question 2:

3. Am I meeting this need currently?
4. If not, what is one thing that I am willing to do differently to meet this need for my spouse?
5. How will my making this effort have a productive impact on our relationship?
6. How might this impact my experience and overall fulfilment as well?
7. When I continue to fulfil my spouse's need, how might the quality of my relationship improve:

a. over the next six months?
b. In a year's time?
c. Over five years or more?

Step 5: Review after a month

Come back to this exercise after thirty days, and notice what you had written down. Now may be a good time to sit down with your spouse to get some feedback. Have a couple's meeting. This is a meeting where each of you takes time out to talk about issues that concern you and your relationship, not about other people, work and so on. Set some ground rules for the meeting beforehand, so that each of you feels safe to speak. Feel free to look at the speaker's/listener's technique in the first book, "*Discover the Best in You!*" for guidance. Work on creating a safe, non-judgmental space for one another.

Ask your spouse if he or she notices a change in the interactions between you. You may now want to share what you have been doing. Ask if it is working for your spouse, so that you get feedback. Even if you already know the pattern has been broken successfully, it can provide an opening for a deeper conversation about what each of you needs and create momentum for an action plan for the next few months.

Case Study: Masuma

Masuma was someone who struck me as a person with a powerful drive to move forward. Now, in her late twenties, she had gotten married young at the age of 19. She had spent the first few years of her marriage focusing on others, but now she wanted to work on other things too. She had several things she wanted to work on including her health, her relationships with her husband and son, as well as wanting to start a new business venture. The one common thread running through her goals was that Masuma felt that her communication skills were lacking.

Masuma was feeling very frustrated in her marriage. Her complaint was that she made requests of her husband that wouldn't be acknowledged by him let alone met. This would lead to frustration on her part. She was a planner, while her husband was much more "in the moment". She also said that he wouldn't open up too much with her.

Through coaching, Masuma began to realize that she wasn't really clear about her own needs. Also she was not framing them directly, so her husband didn't really know what she wanted or needed. For example, she was thinking about bigger things, and wanting to build her life purpose, and she needed her husband's support – but she wasn't asking for it!

She first explored her own needs in various areas of her life. We then worked on how she could communicate her needs. She also realized that she needed to meet some of those herself. She learned to separate between the things she expected of him versus the things she needed to do for herself. With practice, she found that not only was she able to communicate but she was learning to prioritize. For her, the issue was not setting boundaries with her husband but with herself. She was finding it tough to pay attention to her own needs. But now that she was learning to do so her frustrations began to subside, and her relationship with her husband and child improved too.

To Summarize

This chapter focused on exploring specific aspects of marriage, and empowering ourselves to make changes where needed.

- We explored some common assumptions that people make around marriage.
- We explored the differences between assumptions and expectations; we defined what expectations are.
- We explored the idea that we all keep score at an unconscious level; this isn't just around marriage – we keep score in all our relationships!
- We talked about how expectations are masks for what we truly need underneath.
- We talked about how to identify our unmet needs.
- We talked about how to break any pattern that is destructive to the marriage by learning how to understand and focus on what our spouse needs.

7. Overcoming Divorce with Grace

And when you divorce women and they reach their prescribed time, then either retain them in good fellowship or set them free with liberality, and do not retain them for injury, so that you exceed the limits, and whoever does this, he indeed is unjust to his own soul....

Quran 2:231

The best of my community are those who when treated foolishly, are tolerant, and when attacked they forgive, and when they are hurt, are patient.

Prophet Muhammad (pbuh)

Wherever you are now is a good place to start

Let's admit it, divorce is one of the most difficult and traumatic experiences one can go through. Some relationships can be challenging all along. However, it's unrealistic to expect that things will always be smooth sailing, even in strong relationships, they just won't be. I know that this may sound very non-coach-like, but I believe in being authentic. So why are relationships so tough? Well, to be honest, it all boils down to the concept that each human being has a unique point of view. We each experience challenges and carry around invisible leftover baggage to varying degrees. This baggage then impacts how we experience life and how we relate with others. Remember that our past experiences are used to set up expectations for future events; the brain does this automatically. To top it off, we *already* have our own vantage point, so, with baggage added to that, it's no wonder that some of our relationships can be challenging for us.

At times, one may feel so challenged that it feels easier to walk away. If you are still married, but are exploring ending your marriage, then I invite you to look through the chapter on stress, and the chapter on marriage. Give those strategies a go, and I hope that they will give you an opportunity for remedial action – you never know.

This chapter is for those who have already divorced or decided to divorce. Whether you have already ended the relationship, or are in the process of doing so, then the work that we will do in this chapter may well apply to you. *Insha'Allah*, the work we will do here will provide you with some inspiration to make productive changes for the present and for your future. But first we will start with how you are feeling now. Take a few minutes to work through the following questions.

Exercise 7.1: Exploring How I Feel About My Divorce

Outcome: To explore how you are feeling about your breakup as it stands right now.

Method: Answer the questions with the answer that feels most honest to you. This is not to share but is for your own awareness.

- What happened?
- Why didn't it work?
- Whose fault was it?
- What did you or the other person do or not do?
- How are you coping now?

What did you learn by answering these questions? Painful experiences such as divorce compel a person to find reasons as to "why" they happened. We need to make sense of things. Generally, people experiencing this either blame themselves or the other person. Afterall, it is someone's fault, otherwise it wouldn't have happened in the first place, right? Are you blaming yourself, or your ex? Take a moment to reflect on where your emotions currently lie:

On a scale of 1–10, how much are you blaming yourself for the breakup?

1 2 3 4 5 6 7 8 9 10

Not my fault at all | It's all my fault

On a scale of 1–10, how much of the blame belongs to your ex?

1 2 3 4 5 6 7 8 9 10

s/he is totally innocent | It's all his/her fault

Look at your numbers. The two numbers should equal ten if you add them up. Where have you assigned more of the blame? What tells you that this is how it should be divided?

The interesting thing about blame is that it only shows up when something goes wrong. When you reflect, you will notice that credit and blame are two sides of the same coin. Credit is taken or assigned when things are going well. Blame is assigned when things are going wrong. Both credit and blame are forms of accountability, but it's the context that determines which is doled out. The context also determines the emotions that are assigned to that form of accountability. Credit is usually positive and fun, whereas blame is unpleasant and triggers other difficult emotions. It's interesting how our emotions are impacted by our results, isn't it?

Another aspect is that all this negativity occurs because the divorceé feels he or she has failed. The marriage "failed" so the divorcee feels like a "failure". However, we human beings are hardwired to move away from pain. We don't want to feel the pain of being a failure, so we are compelled to assign accountability to the other person. They failed, they didn't measure up, and so the relationship had to end. How closely do you relate to this?

What's your story?

We started this chapter on a heavy note, but things will get lighter. The reason for beginning this way is that we start from where we are. If you have been dealing with a challenging breakup, then it's safe to assume that there will be difficult emotions. The questions above are designed to help you uncover what these are. The next step is to notice that there's a story that's connected to those emotions. Your story is your memory of the events that occurred. What happened, who did what, etc. We have one big life story, and then we have several other stories that fit within this overall framework. It is important to know what story we are holding on to, because this narrative gives rise to our emotions, and gives our experiences meaning.

Open a blank page in your journal and write down your breakup story. What happened during the relationship? What led to the divorce, and your current experience of life at this moment? Take time to notice how you are feeling as you write your story. Notice any negative emotions bubbling up, and just make a little note (next to the story) of how you're feeling as you write about the event. Pay attention to any feelings of failure, guilt, shame, or blaming yourself or the other person.

How much do you share your story?

How does it feel to document your story just for yourself? Do you share your story with people? How often do you share? How do you feel when you relate your story to other people? Does it feel good, as if you are achieving a release, or does sharing your story keep you stuck in the same experience? Upon reflection, you may notice that sharing your divorce story may be keeping you stuck in the very same experiences you're aiming to release. One of most valuable steps you can take is to set some boundaries with yourself about sharing your story. Of course, the temptation will remain, and though the compulsion to feel validated may be a strong one, you have to weigh the pros and the cons of sharing. Take a few minutes to scribble these down:

Table 7.1: The pros and cons of sharing my story

The benefits of sharing my story	The disadvantages of sharing my story
1.	1.
2.	2.
3.	3.
4.	4.
5.	5.

Do the benefits outweigh the disadvantages? What is this sharing giving you? Just imagine that two years have gone by. You have now moved on, but when you run into people that you haven't seen in a long time, you get the sense that they still relate to you as the person you were back then. They look at you with what you experience as pity. How does it feel? One of the biggest cons of sharing too much is that people often remember what was shared – and they begin to relate to you as that person. They don't see the progress that has happened in the time between encounters. If you had shared less, or shared from a productive outlook, that would have been remembered.

One of the most useful things we can do for ourselves is to set boundaries for ourselves to follow. A boundary is setting a guideline for behaviour, for things you will do or not do. First let's get some clarity on how much you're sharing now, and the quality of what you're sharing.

Exercise 7.2: Containing The Share

Outcome: To help you set some boundaries for what you are sharing with others. This can apply to your relationship, or any other area of your life.

Method: Work through the questions below.

Step 1: Awareness

1. Remember the last time you shared your story with someone. Write down 2–3 things you remember telling him or her.
2. On a scale of 1–10, how appropriate was it to share that information? Why?
3. On a scale of 1–10, how safe did you feel after you shared?
4. Did your share allow the recipient to "see" you as you truly are, or did they see a side of you that was not you at your best?
5. How would you like them to relate to you instead?

Step 2: Setting some boundaries

1. What are some things you will now stop sharing? About yourself, your marriage, your divorce/ex, or any other aspects of life?
2. Imagine that you're having a bad day and you feel like venting in a big way. Part of you knows that you're just angry, and it's not a good idea, but if you don't do it, you feel like you will explode. What is one thing that you could do, that would divert your attention from this urge? This could be an ongoing hobby, or something new you've just dreamed of doing. Write it down.

Step 3: Visualize yourself doing it

First of all, only do this exercise when you are feeling good, and there is no sign of negativity. If you're feeling even slightly angry or negative, do not proceed. Do this another time. The aim of this movie is to support you in creating a new pathway of behaviour.

Close your eyes. Imagine you are the star of your own movie. You see everything that is happening – just like you see the world every day. The scene opens and you aren't having the best day. Your ex has managed to aggravate you again. You're just about to call a friend to vent, like you normally do, but you remember this friend will remember it, and ask you about it again and again. So instead of calling her, you decide to do something you love to do. You take a breath, you notice your decision, and then proceed to do what you have chosen to do. Maybe you head out the door, or remain where you are, but the movie continues to unfold. You see yourself doing this activity now. See what you're doing, notice your body language, what you're wearing, your thoughts and anything else. Just take a moment to notice how you grabbed control of the situation, and that urge to vent has melted away. Once the movie is complete, open your eyes. Stand up and give yourself a good shake.

These kinds of visual practices can really help, especially when you're in emotional turmoil. Often, during the early stages of a breakup, the need to vent is very strong. However, sharing can also lead to problems, so this is a great way of being in control. This will then lead to positive sharing. Repeat this exercise every day while you start to engage in more activities you love. These visualizations will support you to take these positive actions in the real world.

Step 4: Clarifying what you want to share
Reflect on what you want to build in your life. Write up to five things you are now creating in your life. These can be goals you're working on already, or things that you are planning for your future. Start building a vision board. Next, reflect on who you want to share your ideas with and why, then go ahead and share! Putting our goals and dreams out there in a productive way supports us by manifesting them.

Why should I control how and what I share?

Imagine that you're going back to visit a place you loved many years ago. I visited the UK after about 5 years away. It was wonderful to visit, but it did feel different than when I lived there. Our minds remember things as snapshots. Our memory of a place or person remains at the point when we last encountered them. No one can account for changes they haven't experienced. So when we go back to that place, or meet that person, the experience often feels different. This is what our emotional memories of situations are like too. The emotion that was felt in that moment shapes the memory. Reflect on a situation that impacted you greatly when it happened, but, if you reflect on it now, it invokes a different feeling. Our feelings depend a great deal on our vantage point. We may feel less intensely or differently about a situation years after the event simply because our circumstances have shifted.

Feelings depend on how you are perceiving a situation at the time. For example, have you ever been to a film with a friend, and each of you reacted completely differently? One loved it and the other hated it. This is because each of you is having a different experience of life right now and each of you holds a unique model of the world.

Turning back to your own story. Again, think of it as if it were a film. There are two main aspects to it. The first is the actual events; the second is your perception of these events. The bare facts don't change, but what you believe or think about these events can shift. Your thoughts and feelings may have little to do with the facts themselves, yet they determine how you experience the event. How you interpret any event either makes you feel good or bad, happy or sad, and so on. So why do we interpret things the way we do? How is it that the facts don't determine our experience? After all, if it was just about the facts, each person would have the same interpretation and experience.

The reason why each person's interpretation varies is because he or she generates his or her own unique model of the world as they go through life. One's unique worldview is shaped by how they were raised, their life experiences, and how they interpreted those experiences. These interpretations, rather perceptions, also have an impact upon one's feelings. By sharing our story, we are repeating those perceptions to others, thereby strengthening our current interpretation of these events. If our perceptions are negative and our story disempowers us, then would it help to strengthen those? No, of course not! This is one important reason to be aware of what we are sharing and to manage it accordingly.

Another reason to raise self-awareness about what we share is to ensure it is not harmful to us or the people concerned. Remember that perceptions are not all accurate, so an inaccurate share may be unnecessarily hurtful for the other person involved, and for ourselves as well. When we share, we are sharing our version of the facts. We *believe* that they are the actual events, but we are always adding our own interpretations to the facts. So essentially, our story is never about objective fact – it is always a personal narrative of how we perceive the facts. This may sound like we are manipulating the story intentionally, but for most of us this isn't the case. We are just sharing what we truly believe happened. We are convinced that our story is the truth. *However,* If the other person were present, he or she might have a very different version of the same events.

Exercise 7.3: Shifting How You Relate To Your Story – Now That's Empowering

Objective: To change how you perceive the story of your breakup

Method: Work through the questions below.

What have you learned about your story so far? Upon reflection, you will notice that it's your own thoughts that activate your feelings. Your experience has less to do with the actions of others. Rather, is it how you're framing events yourself? It may sound harsh to even consider if it's your ex who didn't cause you pain, but it's meant to be empowering. If you can think about yourself negatively, then you can think about yourself positively too! You have perceived the story of your breakup one way, but you can look at it a different way, if you so choose. The new way you perceive it will impact your emotions and the quality of your life on a daily basis. Ask yourself the following questions.

1. On a scale of 1–10, how empowering is my perception of my breakup for me?

1 2 3 4 5 6 7 8 9 10

Not empowering (I feel awful) Totally empowered to move on

2. What am I gaining by keeping my current perception of my breakup alive?
3. What am I losing by keeping this perception (or story) alive?
4. What might I gain by thinking about my story in a different way? Is this gain worth it?
5. On a scale of 1–10, how willing am I to shift my thoughts around my breakup right now?

1 2 3 4 5 6 7 8 9 10

Unwilling Fully willing

If your answer is below a six, then it's likely that you're gaining something valuable by keeping the story alive. There may also be a deeper motivation to keep things the same. If so, then ask yourself why you want to keep this story. Or what's stopping you from letting this story go? Once you know what your deeper motivation is, then you can find another way to meet that need. It will become easier to shift your perspective.

This process may feel difficult but remember you will feel much better when you are successful in shifting your perspective. What would it be like if you could see your situation as an opportunity instead of an ordeal? How could relating to your circumstances differently impact positively upon your health, your productivity, and your quality of life? Shifting our perception is looking at the event through a different lens. Often, it is just about asking a question in a different way. Give the exercise below a try.

Exercise 7.4: Shifting Your Perception Towards Your Breakup

Outcome: To help you shift your perspective so that you can notice opportunities within your situation.

Method: This exercise is divided into sections. Each section begins with the definition of an emotion. Focus on the emotions that apply to you. Go through the relevant sections. Fill in the blanks, or answer the questions as appropriate. You can work through this exercise in any order you wish.

Failure: Getting a result that is contrary to what we hoped or expected to get

My relationship ended, and I feel like I'm a failure because ______________________________________. However, there were many things that were not in my control during the relationship including ____________________. "Failure" is a judgement about a result, but it does not account for the effort that someone puts in. If I look at all my effort, I realize that I truly did ________________________, and that's what really matters.

I know that I did____________________________ so there's no reason to think of myself as "a failure". Instead, I can tell myself that I did all I could have, but got a result that wasn't what I'd hoped for. Instead, what I do have is feedback. Feedback is the information and learning we gain from any experience. The lessons from feedback that I am now taking with me are:

____

And I can now acknowledge that I ____________________________

Shame: A painful feeling of humiliation or distress caused by consciousness of wrong or foolish behaviour

I feel ashamed because ______________________________________

My expectation was that I would be able to ____________________________ but I wasn't able to. This is why I feel so ashamed about the breakup.

Someone could feel ashamed if they did something really terrible, but, if I look back, I notice that I ______________________________ so there's no reason to feel this way. Instead, I now acknowledge myself for ____

Blame: Blaming yourself or someone else means declaring him or her responsible for a fault or wrongdoing.

I'm blaming myself, or my ex, because ____________________ ____________________________. Blaming someone has been giving me ________________ but it's taking away a lot from me too, including______________________. If I take a look, my focus has been on___________________ and if I continue to focus on this, then I may lose opportunities including __________________________. Keeping the blame game alive isn't worth it because______________________________.

Indeed, my ex and I both did things wrong, but if I continue focusing on those mistakes, I will lose _________________________. Maybe it's time to think about those things that were said and done differently. I can now think of those things as ____________ ____. And I am willing to acknowledge myself for ___________________ ____.

Anger: A strong feeling of annoyance, displeasure, or hostility

I feel anger towards myself, or my ex, because _________________ _____________________. I feel so hurt, and disappointed about _______________________ and it's okay for me to feel this way, as hurtful things were said and done. Holding on to this pain gives me _______________________ but it takes a lot away from me including ___________________________. If I truly reflect, it's taking away more than it is giving to me, so maybe it's not the most productive thing to do. What might be more productive is to _______________________________ and focus on something new for the present, and the future of myself and my family. The new attitude that I will focus on now is __________________________, and I am willing to acknowledge myself for ____________________________.

Creating a new story

How was the previous exercise for you? I hope that you have begun to shift your feelings a little bit. Now that you're becoming aware of how your perceptions were impacting you, you can truly take control and begin to shift them for good.

Now it's time to write a new story for the present. Think about all the productive things you are doing to get your life on track. Also reflect on what you would now like to create moving forward. Take a few moments to fill in the table below. Use the example as a guide.

Table 7.2: Reflecting on new actions moving forward

Things that I will be doing differently in the future	**Imagining that I'm doing them right now (from this moment on) and noticing *how* I'm doing them.**
I will be taking care of my own needs as well as the needs of others.	**What**: I am taking care of my own needs, while I take care of others needs as well. **How**: I am looking after the kids, and exercising regularly.
I will pay attention to my tone of voice (how I speak to others).	**What**: I am already paying attention to my tone of voice when I speak to the people who are close to me. **How**: I stop and take three deep breaths each time I feel triggered. It really helps to calm me down.
I will forgive others, and myself, for the mistakes that were made.	**What**: I am practising compassion for myself and others. **How**: I am doing this by writing forgiveness letters whenever I need to.
I will create a fulfilling career or business.	**What**: I am actively creating a new career path for myself. **How**: I've gone back to pursue my degree and am looking for paid internships.

Now visualize

Think about all the things that you are intending to do differently. Pick the three most important to you and focus on them. Create a movie, where the events are unfolding as if you are living through them right now. Imagine a day in your life, as you go about your daily affairs implementing these new actions. Take a moment to allow the movie to run for a minute or so. Open your eyes once you feel that the movie is complete. Repeat this exercise at least once a day over the next month.

This is all well and good, but I still have to deal with my ex!

Well done for creating the shifts in perception that you have achieved so far. However, is your ex's behaviour still winding you up? Though you've tried several times, even thoughts of your ex just seem to wind you up and bring your mood down. Maybe you still have some strong emotions and are have trouble pulling away. You might even find yourself drawn to your ex though the relationship has ended.

Perhaps there are circumstances that keep you connected because you share work, friends, or children. Many people don't have the opportunity for a clean break for whatever reason. If you're one of them, don't despair. There are ways to still have some interaction *and* maintain your wellbeing and sanity at the same time. The first step is to figure out if the amount of interaction you have is necessary, or if the limits are a little bit undefined. Explore the questions below to see if you need to set some clearer limits, either for yourself, or for your ex's interactions with you.

Understanding the current dynamic

1. My ex and I need to remain in contact because of

   ____

2. I am still dependent on my ex for ____________________
   and will continue to remain so for ____________________
3. Choose either a) or b) or both if appropriate:

a. The areas where I need to become independent and stop relying on my ex are:
   -
   -
   -

b. It is not me, instead it is my ex who needs to stop relying on me for:
   -
   -
   -

4. How is this dynamic as "exes" impacting me?

Table 7.3: Exploring the impact of the dynamic

Positive ways this dynamic impacts me	Negative ways this dynamic impacts me

5. The boundaries that remain unresolved between us are:
   a.
   b.
   c.

What did you learn from the preceding exercise? Is it your ex impinging on your life, or is it you who is still quite reliant on your ex? Or are you both still reliant on each other? This is not about judgement – it's about understanding what is going on with you. You need to be aware of what's happening before you can shift it. If you are still reliant on your ex, that's understandable, but it may be impacting you more deeply than you thought. If you feel that it's time to set boundaries (either for your own behaviour or what you will allow your ex to do), then go ahead and work on this. We have worked with boundaries before, so go ahead and use those earlier exercises, or just use the following tips to set some stronger limits. Establishing boundaries becomes easier with practice.

Setting new boundaries

Create a table like the one below, and fill it in. Fill in topics according to what's relevant to you. Examples may include children, money, home maintenance, friends, moral support, family events. The list can be anything you need it to be. Customize this table according to your needs. The aim of it is to support you in establishing new boundaries that you can live with. Note: all of these are for you to do, or not to do. *This is not about your ex.*

Table 7.4: Exploring my new plan to deal with my ex

Topic	Things I am prepared to do for my ex	Things I am no longer going to do for my ex	Things I will no longer lean on my ex for	My new plan	Reminders
Kids at the weekends.	Pick up and drop off the kids on my weekends with them.	Constantly adjusting my plans when he doesn't want to take them.		Create a Google calendar, and stick to it. say *no* when he wants to bail.	
House main-tenance.			Asking him to fix things around the house.	Start a small budget for handyman, or learn DIY.	Put a picture up that inspires me to learn new things.
Moral sup-port.			I rely on him to boost my confidence – I need to stop this.	Make a list of other people I can call. Perhaps find a coach to talk to.	

Summary: In one or two simple, clear sentences, my new plan of action with my ex will be:

Now that you have a new plan, make sure to set some reminders to stay on track. Maybe you need some outside resources, so be sure to get the support you need. Setting firm boundaries sets the context for future communication to create a new dynamic.

What do I do about my feelings?

Sometimes it doesn't even take the person being there for us to feel sad or upset. Just thinking about them can bring up a lot of feelings. The mind is so powerful because it does so many things without us even trying. The first thing it naturally does, is that it creates little markers that associate events with feelings. Once a certain feeling has been associated with a certain type of event, an event that feels similar will trigger similar feelings. For example, if someone received the silent treatment due to bad behaviour as a kid, they will instantly feel those same feelings when their spouse or colleague doesn't speak to them. It just could be that they are busy, but the person will feel the same original sense of abandonment. This holds true for associating good feelings too.

The second thing our minds do is that they don't always differentiate between reality and imagination. So even when you imagine your ex, or think of them, it's no surprise that the same feelings are triggered. The feelings will feel as vivid as if your ex was right in front of you, and the event was happening in real time at that very moment.

It's perfectly normal and understandable to feel upset, angry, sad or a sense of longing, whether you're thinking about, or interacting with your ex. The way to reduce those feelings is to tie another feeling to that memory, essentially replacing the feelings associated with your ex. So for example, if you feel angry each time you interact with your ex, think about how you would like to feel instead. Once you have this alternative feeling, you will then need to create a new association in your mind. The association of emotions with an event, person, words, a sound, etc. is called an "anchor" in NLP jargon. Just think of it as a memory hook if you prefer. An example of an anchor for me is a very specific song. Each time I've heard it playing on the radio, it takes me to a very vivid memory of spending time with my dad when I was very little. Think of a certain song, smell, food, or item of clothing, etc. that immediately triggers a memory or experience for you – that is an anchor. In the same way, you may have developed certain very strong anchors during your relationship. Now that you've split up, interacting with your ex, or certain objects, words, behaviours, etc. can trigger the anchor. Therefore, you find yourself feeling the same way you did before. This is about recognizing, and not just realising, this is happening. Do the following exercise if you would like to be in a more empowering emotional state while interacting or dealing with your ex.

Exercise 7.5: Anchoring A New Feeling

Outcome: To remove a negative trigger of your ex.

Method: This exercise has two phases. Phase 1 is about clarity, the second is about anchoring. Make sure to read all the instructions in Phase 2 before starting it.

Phase 1: Awareness
Each time I think about, or communicate with my ex, I end up feeling ______________________

Step 1: Choosing the instance
Recall up to three instances that caused you to feel the same way when interacting with your ex. Write down each incident along with one or two words about the associated feelings. Use the example as a guide.
Example: My ex did not show up on his designated day to spend with the kids. (anger, resentful, insulted.)

1.
2.
3.

Pick the one that is the most vivid or, emotional for you and work with it.

Step 2: Finding an alternative emotional state
Think about how you would like to feel instead, each time you interact with them. This is your desired feeling and state. Come up with three alternatives, then choose the most inspiring one.

Examples: calm and collected, confident, firm and clear.

Choose the one that's the most compelling. Fill it in using the template below:
I intend to be _____________ when interacting with my ex.

Example: I intend to be calm and collected when interacting with my ex.

Step 3: Experiencing the new emotional state
Recall a time when you were the way you now wish to be. For example, if it's calm and collected, then remember a time when you were calm so that you have a reference point. Reflect on what you were doing, saying, or your body language. Visualise yourself in this state – the clearer the words and image, the better. Once you have a clear picture and idea of how you are in this new desired state, then continue to Phase 2. Remember that if this is a completely new behaviour you want to implement, then try practising it in other situations so that you get used to how it feels. Get a sense of how it would work, and then move on to your next step.

Phase 2: Establishing a new anchor
Please read these instructions carefully before continuing. Anchoring is quick, but it takes place in 3 distinct steps. Read the whole process before starting. In Step 1, you will create a new anchor. In Step 2, you will visualize from the coach's position. And in Step 3, you will fire up your new anchor.

Step 1: Reflect on Step 3 from Phase 1

Bring that image back to mind. Close your eyes and imagine yourself in this state when you were calm, or whatever it is you want to anchor. Imagine this picture as clearly as you can. Take a deep breath and feel the feeling inside your body. When you are sure that it's strong, then clench your fist (whichever you prefer) for a moment. When the feeling is truly there inside you, just absorb it for a moment, then open your eyes and let go. Repeat this process 3–5 times, or as many times as required until that feeling is strong. This is you establishing this new physical and emotional state as an anchor.

Step 2: Reflect on Step 1 from Phase 1

Choose the instance that is the most vivid in your mind, and bring it up. Run a movie in your mind where you are seeing the events unfold as an observer. Imagine you are in a cinema watching your own story like it's someone else's story. As you watch the screen, you observe yourself getting triggered, but you notice that you're responding with your new chosen state – in a calm and collected way and so on. Notice what you're doing, your posture, your body language, your words, etc. See yourself being successful. When the scene is over, open your eyes.

Get up from your position, move around a little bit. Give your body a good shake! Please make sure to do this as it's important.

Step 3: Test out your new anchor

Recall again the very same incident. This time, you will run the movie as if it is happening right now. You are experiencing the event first-hand, and *not* as an observer. It is taking place just as it did before, but when you clench your fist, you step into your newly empowered state. Examine how you are responding this time. Notice how positive feelings have replaced what was there previously. Take time for the incident to unfold, all the while taking in how you're now interacting differently. Note your words, posture, body language and anything else. Once the incident is complete, open your eyes. Move around and shake your body again.

Step 4: Practice

The coaching term we use to activate an anchor is to "fire" it. Take a few minutes every day to practise firing this anchor. You can just visualize the state as you did in Step 2, or you can do Step 3. What might be even more powerful is to clench your fist at the very first sign of those feelings. Use this tool in any situation that requires it, so this new state becomes more firmly established within. Whenever you feel the old negative trigger, just go ahead and clench your fist. Remind yourself of what it is to be in your new desired state. The more you use it, the better established the new anchor will become. With practice, the new feelings will become automatic. Your mind will create new associations for this wonderful state. In time, you may not even notice falling into the new state and not having to clench your fist at all.

Let's summarize the main points

A breakup or divorce is not easy, so our aim was to empower you to get through the process as best you can. The most important concept to remember is that it is one's own story and interpretation of events that forms one's experiences. Therefore, our focus was not on your ex, but on you creating a more empowering narrative for your experience and life overall. The main areas that we covered included:

- Exploring your current experience of your breakup.
- Gaining awareness of how sharing your experience can impact you.
- Learning how much to share, and in what way.
- Learning to let go of blame and other negative emotions.
- Understanding your current story, and creating a new narrative of your experience.
- Setting clear boundaries for yourself when interacting with your ex.
- Creating a new anchor for old triggers – so that you can behave in a whole new way around your ex and in your life in general.

8.
Stress Stresses Relationships

Do people think that they will be let go
merely by saying: "We believe," and that
they will not be tested?

Qur'an 29:2

'Blessed are the sincere. They are the lanterns
of guidance, and all dark trials are cleared
away from them.'

Prophet Muhammad (pbuh)

Many of us suffer from chronic stress nowadays, and our stress definitely spills onto our relationships, doesn't it? This is primarily because we are feeling anxious or in a state of "dis-ease." Have you ever snapped at a loved one without meaning to? For example, it's the middle of the afternoon, and you come home to find a major leak in the kitchen. You run to shut off the water and start making frantic calls to get a plumber in. As you're doing this, your 4-year-old son comes over to you and says, "Mum, can I have some ice cream, please, please, please, Mum?" Instead of handling your 4-year-old as you normally would, you snap at him, "Shut up! Can't you see I'm on the phone?" He leaves the room sobbing, and you feel like the worst parent in the world!

Can you relate to this example? Pretty much all of us have snapped at someone, said something unpleasant, or reacted in anger from time to time. What did you tell yourself when you did so? Did you blame the other person for provoking you? However, if you looked deeper, you might notice it was something else that was bothering you.

Of course, there are times when someone says or does something hurtful. However, most people rarely have such extreme reactions to a simple request or a minor annoyance. Consider that such outbursts are caused by lingering stress. The last event was just a trigger. When stress gets to be at a certain level, we may respond in extreme ways. Therefore, an outburst is seen as unreasonable by other people. They won't know the overreaction is triggered by underlying stress.

What is stress?

Stress can either be useful or destructive because we experience different kinds of stress. At certain times stress can be helpful, but it can be destructive to our wellbeing and our relationships.

Recall a time when you were competing in a sporting event or giving a presentation. Did you feel nervous beforehand? Did you find yourself going red, maybe feeling shaky or jittery, had sweaty palms, but once you began all the "nerves" went away? That would be an example of "good" stress. Now remember a time where you experienced "bad" stress. Maybe you were late for a work deadline, or there was an emergency with a family member. What were your symptoms then?

You will notice that the physical symptoms you experienced were similar in both instances. This is surprising but is also an invaluable insight. Namely, that our bodies only have one physiological mechanism for handling any kind of stress. However, what makes stress "good" or "bad" is the nature of our thoughts about the situation we are in. If you're planning for a stage performance, or whether you're dealing with a leak at home, the physical symptoms might be the same, but the thought behind it will be very different.

A negative focus on the "other"

Any relationship can work when both parties maintain a *positive* and *productive* focus towards each other. Think of one of your most valued relationships. It could be a friend, a family member, or a colleague. Where is your focus when you think of this person whom you hold a lot of love and respect for? If you notice, you will see that your focus is on the other person. You may recall some good memories, you may think of their positive qualities, some of the things that they do. You hold a positive and productive picture of them in your mind, and your emotions match that picture.

Just imagine that you have been very stressed for some time. Something big has gone wrong, and this life-altering event has been consuming all your energy. You reach out to this person for help, but he or she has been disappointing you lately. The very person who was there for you before is unavailable now. Bring this person to mind. Where is your focus now? Perhaps it's on your own disappointment and hurt. The positive image doesn't come up. You probably can come up with a quick list of all the times they have disappointed you. But wait a moment, take a breath and absorb what I'm about to say.

Stress impacts us in such a profound way that it changes how we perceive everything! This has to do with how the brain is built, but neurobiology is not our focus here. What's important to know is that stress releases chemicals designed to deal with momentary threat or challenge. The part of our brains that holds the ability to be creative and think critically is inhibited.

When the traumatic event has passed, we may feel that we are over the stress, but lingering effects may remain. Recall a time when the stressful event had passed, but you still didn't quite feel like yourself. Write down three things that just didn't feel the same:

1. ______________________________
2. ______________________________
3. ______________________________

The residual impact of stress shows up in our day-to-day life. For example, food may not taste as good, the usual pastimes aren't fun, people whom we normally enjoy spending time with irritate, and so on. Coaching in such circumstances is useful because it clears away these residual emotions. Not only do we learn to cope with trauma, but we also take new lessons, and can integrate them into our current life experience; this is what helps us create lasting changes.

Think of stress as a state of "dis-ease." We are calling it "dis-ease" because we literally feel a lack of ease when stress hormones are coursing through our bodies. The **fight–flight–freeze** response gets triggered in our brains as a reaction to danger. Once triggered, hormones are released and we experience the rapid heartbeat, taut muscles and so on. They help either fight, flee and freeze in a dangerous situation – and we need our bodies primed for this in an instant.

We should realize this system is essential for survival. There are times when we need to react instantly. Imagine if we couldn't swerve the car if something is coming the other way, we would perish. Yet, the fight–flight–freeze response cannot distinguish a physical threat and an emotional one. It interprets all "threats" the same way. We will be ready to fight in the same way whether we are being attacked by a lion or our boss said something inappropriate. The physical effects are the same, and, before we know it, we are primed to attack the boss! Therefore, some arguments can escalate without warning.

Most of us face stresses that are emotional in nature. If someone experiences chronic stress, they respond to how they feel in the moment. They are unable to reflect on the big picture, or larger consequences in that instant. If something else happens at the same time, that will be enough to trigger an angry outburst because the underlying threat mechanism is already activated, and an argument may well ensue.

A stressed person is not able to see the bigger picture. They are not able to notice what might be the other person's reality or intention. Imagine you are dealing with someone experiencing chronic stress. Even though you may not have meant anything by it, the stressed person senses your words as threatening. This is why you experience him or her as lashing out in anger. The opposite is also true. If we are stressed, we experience the other person's words as threatening, when they are not meant to be.

We have a bit of a problem here. The chronic stresses we face these days may damage our relationships if we don't do something about them. We can't alter our physiology, but we can learn to identify stress and deal with it in a different way. The key is awareness. Awareness plays a huge role in helping us clean out the residual impacts of stress, as well as allowing our creative side to come back into play. Awareness works to rebalance our systems. Stress may still be there, but, through awareness, we manage stress without it negatively affecting our relationships.

The first step is to understand how we are currently responding to stress. Once we are aware what's happening right now, we can shift our behaviour. Take some time to observe your own behaviour under stress.

Exercise 8.1: Observing Your Own Behaviour Under Stress

Outcome: To help you observe how you react under stress.
Method: Answer the questions in your coaching journal.

Recall a time when you got angry, or maybe yelled at someone who is important to you.

1. Describe the event. What happened?
2. What did you say and do?
3. How did the other person react? Did he or she also get angry (if it's your child, did he or she answer back?)
4. What was the impact on the relationship at that time?
5. What impact is still present?
6. Was this event a one-off, or has it become a pattern of behaviour?
7. What behaviour should you take accountability for?

Stress is a response to triggers

Physical threats aside, modern life leaves us stressed most of the time. We don't even realize it, but this dis-ease has become our permanent way of experiencing life. Furthermore, being stressed out over a long period of time can wreak havoc on both our health and the quality of our relationships.

If this sounds familiar, remind yourself that you're doing your best. You have a demanding life, so just take a moment to practise some self-compassion. If a specific incident where you said or did something unpleasant is nagging at you, then make a note of it right now. I invite you to resolve to apologize and go ahead with that as soon as you can. This will set the tone for your work ahead.

Now coming back to stress. Stress is a reaction to a trigger. Unexpected events, an argument, or an illness are all triggers. Any number of situations causes this state of dis-ease. Any situation where we feel threatened or vulnerable may trigger stress. Even loved ones behaving out of the ordinary can trigger it. Let's imagine our mother-in-law says something hurtful, and, before you know it, you've reacted angrily. These emotional overreactions are often instantaneous, but they only do further damage. Instead, let's look at a more productive way to handle stress, anger or upset. Give the following exercise a go.

Exercise 8.2: Exploring An Option

Outcome: To brainstorm alternative behaviours to handle stress in a more empowering way. This exercise addresses those stresses and frustrations you face regularly.

Method: Just follow the steps and make notes as you go along.

Step 1: Identify the triggers
Think of five common situations that cause you to feel frustrated or angry. Think of these as your triggers or "pet peeves". These can even be your own behaviours, as sometimes we do tend to frustrate or anger ourselves. Avoid general scenarios and be as specific as possible.

I feel angry/frustrated when (for example: I don't manage my time; my husband leaves dirty dishes in the sink; my child is uncooperative; my boss micromanages me, etc.)

1. ____________________
2. ____________________
3. ____________________
4. ____________________
5. ____________________

Step 2: Observation

Reflect on the last three times when your buttons were pushed. These could include the scenarios you listed above. Try to recall very specific instances of these scenarios. Explore one specific event at a time. Run through the event in your mind, and recall what happened, and how you reacted. Fill in the blanks for each situation, one at a time. The goal here is to figure out a common pattern. Then repeat for the next situation.

When I feel frustrated or angry, I ____________________

____

My tone of voice is ____________________________

____

I say ______________________________________

____

I do _______________________________________

____

Once I've calmed down, I then __________________

____

I am left feeling _____________________________

____

What is the common pattern that you are you noticing? Be as specific with the "story" as possible, using your answers above.

Example

When I feel angry, I raise my voice. My tone is frustrated, and I say something in a loud voice. I use hand gestures and roll my eyes. I'm told off by the other person, and then, once I calm down, I end up apologizing. But I am left feeling upset and more damage is done to the relationship.

If you could change one thing about how you behave, what would that be?

Step 3: Looking for alternatives
You can now plan alternatives for when your buttons get pushed the next time. This step takes place in two stages. Stage 1 is about brainstorming alternatives, and stage 2 is about visualizing the desired outcome.

Stage 1: Planning alternative actions

Be clear about your pattern before proceeding. Bring it to mind, and then ask yourself, "What are three things would I do differently the next time I feel triggered, or sense that it's about to happen again?"

Examples
I can leave the room for a few minutes to calm down.
I can request some alone time or leave the room.
We can agree upon a discreet "take a breath" signal for when an interaction is going downhill for either of us.

What are three new specific and clear behaviours, if different from the above examples, that I might take on?

1. ______________________________
2. ______________________________
3. ______________________________

How convenient are these to implement? How might these new behaviours impact me, and my loved ones, in a more productive way?

Stage 2: Visualization

It's time to visualize the new behaviour. Visualization strengthens the chances of implementation because our mind–body system feels familiarity with the new behaviour. Choose the new behaviour you are most drawn to. Recall the desired outcome when you've handled a situation productively.

Close your eyes and imagine that you are starring in a movie about your situation. The movie begins. You see yourself as angry or triggered. The situation unfolds and you're handling it using your new behaviour. You're experiencing this first-hand. You sense your body language, your words, your tone of voice, etc. See your loved ones, how you are now responding to them, and take your time to notice all the details that are coming up. Allow yourself to fully engage with the movie. When you've visualized the new result, and the movie has reached a natural conclusion, take a few moments, and then open your eyes.

Final step

Think of one inspiring word that describes this new behaviour. Write it down on big pieces of paper and place it in a few locations where you normally spend time through the course of the day. It could be on your bedroom wall, on your computer or phone screen, or in your office. It will serve as a reminder. When you see this word, it is an opportunity to close your eyes and run the movie. Run your movie at least once during the day. Remember, it need only take a minute. This way the new alternative will really begin to become the new course of action.

Learning to break the pattern

What did you notice while doing the previous exercise? You may have learned about how you "do" stress. We all "do" stress differently. Not all of us get angry or shout. Some people become very quiet, some ruminate, some sulk. We're all different and it's vital to recognize our own personal triggers, and how we behave when our buttons get pushed.

The behaviours we carry out repeatedly form a pattern within the mind–body system. Something done occasionally retains its newness. A habit, however, is a pattern that has been repeated so often that the mind has formed a firm pathway for it. It has become an instant and unconscious habit. Driving a car is a great example. Once someone has mastered the art of driving, they seem to do it automatically. They don't think about each step, do they? We have lots of behaviours that we do daily but hardly notice any more. Think of five things that you do well.

1. ________________________
2. ________________________
3. ________________________
4. ________________________
5. ________________________

How does it feel to notice things that you're doing well? Good, right? Remember that these habits are patterns, things that you've done enough times that your mind has absorbed it. However, habits that are induced by stress are also patterns. The great thing about patterns is that they work automatically, without much conscious effort on our part. The key is that we want good patterns to be firmly established, and somehow break the unproductive ones. The good news is that patterns can be broken! And it isn't as difficult as one might think. It takes two things to break a pattern. The first is understanding what the pattern is and the second is to interrupt the pattern in the middle by doing something different!

By now, you probably have at least one alternate way of behaving differently during stressful moments. Hopefully, you have already started using it and getting results. An alternate behaviour is a great way to start exploring options and raising awareness, but there may be a potential issue there as well. The issue is that this alternative may only work if you are aware during that moment and can engage in the new behaviour consciously. This would be wonderful if implemented, but stress often causes us to react. Alternatives require conscious effort, whereas reactions are instantly triggered. So even though you may have firm resolve, the alternative may not work completely. It may not work at all for the first few times. However, the more you engage with it, the easier it will become to implement.

So even though you're working on alternatives, stressful situations demand that you enact a change quickly. Patterns fire within seconds, so the whole behaviour may have happened before you even realize what occurred. For example, you may have already shouted at your 4-year-old before realizing you were stressed about something else. Running the pattern means the behaviour cycle has been completed – you've been triggered, had the stressful outburst, and then calmed down. Wouldn't it be wonderful if you could break that pattern at any point, so even if the argument has started, it can end in a better way?

This would mean that you've interrupted the pattern, so even if it started it didn't get completed as it did before. A pattern can be interrupted by doing something, anything small, differently. Here is an exercise that will allow you to notice where you can break the pattern.

Exercise 8.3: Breaking The Pattern

Outcome: To find ways to break an unproductive pattern. First use this exercise to work on any patterns regarding stress, and you can then use it for other personal habits as well.

Method: Fill in the blanks or answer the questions. Take your time with this process. Note down any new things that come up and be sure to document them as you go along.

Begin with a situation such as a recurring argument with a loved one that, when resolved, will improve the quality of both your lives, for example, about finances, or how to parent children, etc.

Step 1: Notice the hot topics

Think about the key people who are most impacted by your stress. Recall certain recurring situations that impact the quality of your life. Recall the event, noting specific details in how it unfolds. Notice the impact it leaves behind. You may choose to work on the situation from the previous exercise, or work on another situation. Do what feels right to you in the moment.

The main topics that we argue about are ______________________

____

You might notice some of the things that you documented in the previous exercise, namely, the things that push your buttons.

Step 2: Visualize the sequence

Recall the last big argument you had. Bring it to mind and visualize it as if you are watching a movie. You are replaying your memory of the event. Notice the sequence of events as they occurred. What happened first? Who said and did what? The aim is to notice the general pattern and not necessarily the specific subject.

Once you are done with the movie, then document all that you noticed. Write it down in bullet form, so that you can note the sequence of events as you remember them happening.
The sequence of the argument usually is:

The trigger ________________________________
First step in the argument ________________________
Second step in the argument ______________________
Third step in the argument ________________________
Fourth step in the argument ______________________
Fifth step in the argument ________________________
Sixth step in the argument (till you complete the sequence)

Note: if you feel that your notes are about a specific event that doesn't reflect the general pattern as such, then go back and choose another more typical incident that occurred recently or further back in time. There will be a general pattern as to how the arguments go, that's the important thing to discern and work with.

Step 3: How do I break the pattern?

This part of the exercise is crucial, so take time to do it thoroughly. Draw a copy of the diagram below in your notebook. Now that you have an idea of how things go, select one common situation to work with. Document each step of the pattern. Then go back and assess which one thing you could do differently. Look for something that will potentially break the pattern at each stage so that the argument dissipates. Do not worry if you do not find six steps, but do make sure to note all the major steps in the pattern.

Diagram 8.1: Exploring the steps in the pattern

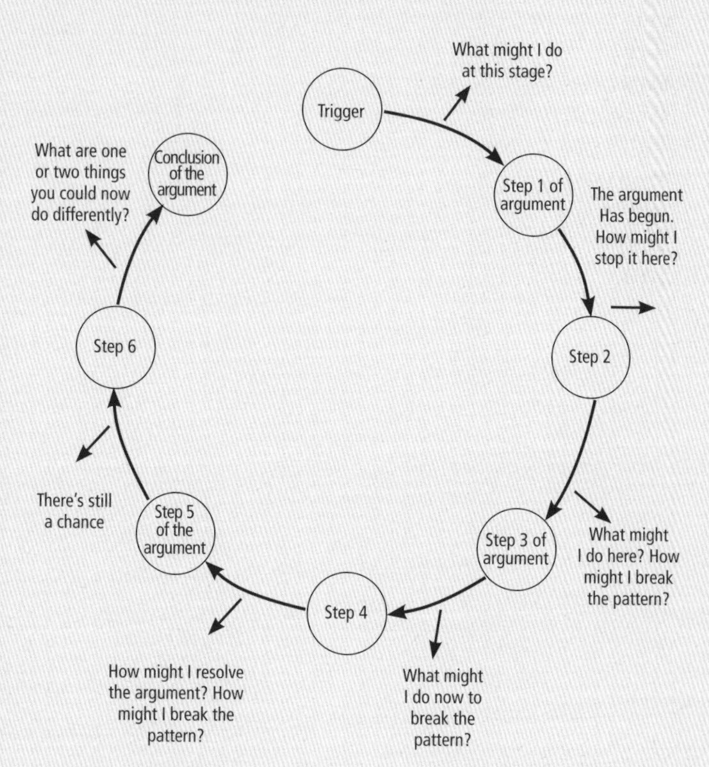

Step 4: Observations

What are one or two things you could now do differently?
How will these actions break the pattern?
Which of these actions are you willing to try out?

Step 5: Reminders!

Commit to one new action that breaks the pattern should an argument be triggered. Come up with key words to describe it, for example, "silence", "breathing", "touch", and so on. Use words that accurately describe the action.

I invite you to find images or photographs that will serve as instant visual reminders (the unconscious mind responds to visual cues). Place your reminders where you can see them. Remember that triggers happen quickly so you won't have time to look for the reminders at that point.

If you want to take it even further, take a few minutes to visualize yourself in a movie. You and another person have gotten into an argument. See yourself breaking this negative pattern effectively using your new strategy. Practice this visualization every few days to remind yourself to use the new strategy.

Patterns are automatic

You've probably noticed how stress impacts an important relationship in your life. Let's reflect on its context for a moment. Are you both having the same argument over and over? The topics may change but consider that the behaviour dynamic is following a pattern. Stress is often triggered by our own limiting beliefs showing up in our interactions with others. As our beliefs don't shift by themselves, it means that the way you will handle stress in that relationship won't change either. This results in the pattern repeating itself.

If you aren't clear about your pattern yet, take another hot topic and work through the previous exercise. Note the pattern in how things play out. When you detect that the pattern is repeating itself, then you know that you're on the right track. Even though the hot topic may vary, the pattern will remain the same. A pattern is essentially a habit. We all have habits for a variety of things, including the way we argue with a loved one.

It may not always seem like it, but the fact that human behaviours follow patterns is a wonderful thing. This is how we form all our habits, both productive and unproductive ones. Imagine if we couldn't establish patterns? We wouldn't be able to do the hundreds of things we do on autopilot.

Once established, habits seem difficult to break. Therefore, we face challenges in giving up smoking, losing weight, etc. Some patterns may seem more challenging to break than others for two reasons. The first is that we aren't fully aware of the pattern, and the second is that the habit meets a deeper need. Some behaviours require that we meet the need in another way, but as we have talked about that previously, so we won't focus on it here.

Let's focus instead on the behaviours that we don't want to keep, but whose patterns have become hard to "see" and break. Frequent arguments with someone may be one of them. It may be that we can't see a way out of it.

The key to being able to break the pattern is to perceive it. As you notice the beginning, middle and end of how a conflict plays out, you can spot opportunities where the pattern can be interrupted. Once you understand the pattern, you can interrupt it when the argument is triggered. This is why reminders are so useful but keeping them simple and easy is crucial. Take a look at the following tips.

Tips for choosing a powerful reminder

- Choose one or two powerful keywords that will remind you to act in this new way.
- Choose visual aids (photos, drawings, etc.) that achieve the same purpose.
- Have both images and words – give your mind a choice.
- Remember the reminders need to work fast – so choose something compelling.
- Visualize yourself acting in this new way – at least once a day!
- Stay hopeful and keep doing something different till you find what breaks the pattern!

Conflicts trigger our survival mechanism

You should have a good idea about what your own triggers and stress patterns are by now. If you still feel unclear about what's triggering you, or how the pattern plays itself out, then take your time with the above exercises before moving on. Remember there is no rush. Typically, we are so immersed in our own patterns that they are difficult to see. It's much easier to see another person's pattern than our own – this is because it takes an observer's perspective to achieve this clarity. Be kind to yourself and continue working towards greater self-awareness.

It might feel like every situation is initially different, but once you start observing, you tend to notice repeat patterns of behaviour in situations *that feel alike*. Stress is stress, whether it be work, financial, or family-related. If the go-to behaviour is to get defensive or worked up, then this pattern will show itself in the different contexts of one's life.

Just recall the last time you were stressed, and inadvertently took it out on someone you love. Recall the event, and how you reacted. Whether a stress-induced argument is about money, in-laws, or child upbringing, what truly matters is to understand that this is a stress pattern running itself; a pattern that's been created by all the people involved interacting together.

Recall the most recent conflict. How did you feel at the start, during and after the interaction? What made the argument escalate? Maybe the other person said something, and you reacted? The important thing to notice is *why* you reacted. How did you feel, that *caused you* to react? What are you noticing now?

What caused me to react was that I felt______________________________

Were you feeling vulnerable in some way? Vulnerability is essential to form a deep bond, but stress and vulnerability can be a dangerous combination. Let's try to understand this from a physiological point of view.

We've already talked about the fact that our mind–body system has a built-in mechanism to respond to threatening stimuli. However, the fight–flight–freeze system doesn't distinguish between physical and emotional threat. This mechanism will be triggered whether the threat is actual (physical) or perceived (emotional). It is automatic and unconscious; it is designed to help us survive.

If it were a physical threat, then we would have lots of energy to fight or flee from the situation. You might have heard of certain heroic acts from people in dangerous situations; that's fight–flight–freeze helping them survive or save others. However, if the stress is of an emotional nature, then we will go into our default strategy of dealing with emotional "threats".

Once fight–flight–freeze has been triggered, then its job will be to help us defend ourselves. All non-essential biological processes will be shut down, including our access to creativity and problem-solving. In that moment, all we will be aware of is our need to survive this "threat". We will react to everything as a threat, even it's not intended in that way. For example, a couple are having a disagreement about going on a holiday, and the wife says something like, "I wish you were around more." Immediately the husband responds, "You're never happy. It's impossible to please you, no matter what I do!" She may have meant that she is missing him, but what he heard was that he is not enough, or not doing enough.

Can you think of a time when you reacted severely? When you reflect, *you notice that you reacted harshly because you felt threatened in some way.* Indeed, there is a biological system at work here. It may be instinct to react insensitively, or in anger, if you're feeling attacked. However, just imagine you continue to do so every time you are stressed. How will this stressed behaviour impact your relationships in the long run?

What constitutes a "threat" depends on an individual's own life experiences. Your reactions provide you with valuable feedback about your own "trigger points". Let's take a general example to understand this. There's a couple who've been married for a very long time. Each disagreement triggers old baggage for the wife. She starts blaming her husband for all the terrible things his family have done to her. He reacts by defending himself and his family. He reminds her of all the helpful things his family have done for her, but they just continue to blame each other. She might have started out as a victim in the argument, and somehow pushed her husband to be the aggressor. Psychiatrist Stephen Karpman explains that all human beings tend to fall into a triangle of three roles each time they are in conflict. This is a general pattern of how people are "being" when they are in conflict. Look at the diagram below:

Diagram 8.2: The Drama Triangle

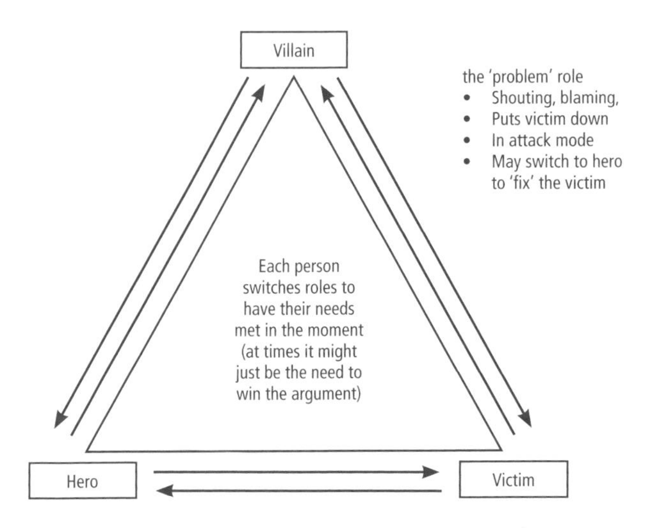

- I'm so good
- I'm helping you (the victim)
- Can be condescending
- Prevents the victim from growing
- Can push the other person into 'victim'mode
- Can be the martyr
- Come across as sacrificing then be pushed into victim

- Poor me
- You're always blaming me
- Its not all my fault
- No one understands me
- Victim 'tries' hard and becomes hero role
- Victim may want to defend and counter a Hack hence becoming the villian

The roles we play in the blame game

If you look this up, you will see this diagram commonly referred to as the Drama Triangle. Think of this as the vicious cycle we all unconsciously fall into when we're in conflict with someone. This happens primarily because we feel attacked and feel compelled to defend ourselves. This is unconscious and automatic.

It's not as if we have a choice. If threat is sensed, the fight–flight–freeze mechanism will kick in. Before we know it, we are pulled into an argument and the blame game begins. The point then becomes to prove oneself the innocent victim, while the other person is the aggressor. Once we are sucked in by this, everyone loses. There's pain, disconnection and further baggage put on the relationship. Remember that this is automatic, and a default way of being. However, this can be shifted with awareness. Note that it's easier to recognize the role someone else is in – primarily because we can't notice when we are in it ourselves. Therefore, developing an objective awareness is essential, so that next time we can catch ourselves doing it. Let's take a look at how these three roles play out:

1. **The victim** is the one defending himself. He could be blaming the other person (the villain) for something. The victim will feel that he has been mistreated, misunderstood, pressurized, etc.

2. **The villain** is the one who is "the problem". He isn't listening or trying to understand. He's the one shouting or acting cruelly. When we are in victim mode, we are pushing the other person into becoming "the villain". We may also switch from being the victim to the villain; we may also counter-attack.

3. **The hero** is the one who shows how good we are, that we are actually helping the victim out. This role can be seen as condescending to the other person.

Emotional stress often leads to conflict because we get triggered and sucked into one of these three roles. We may begin as the victim, and push the other person to be the villain, and so on. Our default starting role will be determined by our upbringing, personal baggage etc. We take on that role, and automatically project the other person into one of the other roles. If the other person moves roles, so do we – and this is how the dance continues, with us hopping between roles. Reflect on the last argument you had. Which role did you begin with? Were you the hero or the victim? Did you feel that you were being treated badly, or did you just want to help, but were misunderstood? What are you noticing about the role you end up being the most often? Take a few minutes to explore this below.

Observation of my default role

Each time _____________ (name colleague, friend, loved one) and I argue, I usually feel like the ______________________________________
I know that I am the _______________ because I usually say___________________ and do ___________________ while the other person ____
The role s/he usually pushes me into is the role of the _______________________. Once pushed into this role, I react and say something like ____
The argument ends by ____________________________________
The roles we end the argument on are with me as ______________ and the other as ____

The impact of this dynamic on our relationship is that ______________
____

How are you left feeling at the end of the interaction? Did you defend yourself sufficiently? Do you feel that you overcame the threat? fight–flight–freeze is very useful when we are dealing with physical threats. However, it's highly problematic when triggered in times of emotional threat. The aim becomes to defend yourself, and to "win" over the emotional threat, but you end up losing because the relationship is damaged in the process.

The unfortunate part is that no one would do this on purpose, would they? You may not even recognize that you've been triggered. To add to this, another huge problem with being in fight–flight–freeze mode is that any access to creativity and change is immediately shut down. There is a disconnect between the executive brain and the part that's driving these emotional responses. You inadvertently attack because you need to survive, and all it does is drives a bigger wedge in your relationship.

So what do we do?

What have you discovered so far? Are you playing the blame game when you're stressed? Are the triggers emotional or coming from elsewhere? Remember there could be environmental factors contributing to your stress such as lack of sleep, overwork, illness, etc. These can make us feel more vulnerable and threatened. Remember that you're only human, so be compassionate with yourself. Now that you have this awareness, there is something you can do.

Imagine if you changed the way that you respond and chose another role? What would that be like? What if this change shifted the conflict's dynamic? You might be thinking that both people must change roles, but that's untrue. If you shift how you respond, the other person's response will naturally shift, and change will happen anyway. The most powerful way of changing the dynamic is to shift our own role within it. Take a moment to reflect on three different and more empowering roles, other than hero, villain or victim, that you could take on. What might they be?

1. ____________________
2. ____________________
3. ____________________

With awareness comes choice. Truth be told, it can be virtually impossible to turn a stressful situation around, just in that charged moment. However, with proactive awareness, and practice, the unconscious mind may be able to access this new behaviour when we most need it. What would it be like to transform a normally stressful situation into a more meaningful connection? What if you could fulfil your desired outcome of being a companion, a supporter, a guide, or a friend? So let's look at the same triangle now, but with different possibilities:

Diagram 8.3: New possibilities to break the Drama

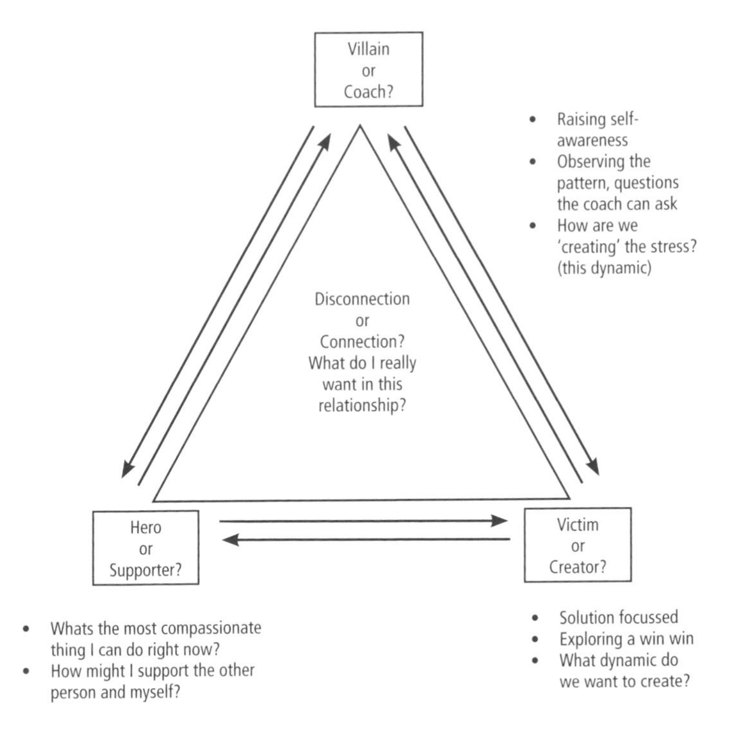

Let's look at the new options instead.

Supporter

This is the role where we genuinely support the other person, and even ourselves. There are some questions we can ask ourselves. How might I support myself and the other person right now? What's the most compassionate thing I can do right now?

Coach

This role is about creating space for clarity and awareness for all concerned. It can be tricky to step into the coach's position when emotions are running high because you may still feel triggered. Remember the coach's role is about asking the right questions while being impartial and compassionate. Take time out, allow things to calm down, then ask yourself the following questions. Do this before you ask them of the other person.

What is our specific pattern? How do we create stress with one another? What is one thing we can do differently, especially during moments of tension or stress? Are there any unexamined issues that we need to discuss and resolve? What are three things we can do to enhance our communication with one another?

Creator

This can be the most enjoyable role, because you get to create something different. Stepping into this role means that you're willing to look for solutions, and to approach the glass as half-full. Take some time to explore a possible win-win solution between you and the other person. Here are some useful questions to ask.

What kind of work, friendship, or relationship dynamic do we want to create together? How might we empower one another to manage our stress more effectively? In situations, where we disagree, how might we find a win-win solution that works for both of us?

We discussed creating a win-win solution in my first book, *Discover the Best in You!*, so it might be useful to have a look at that section if you have it. Essentially, a win-win is a dynamic where both parties feel they get something of value. Most conflicts leave at least one person feeling like he or she lost. This creates a win-lose dynamic. The loser eventually gets fed up of losing and resentments build up, resulting in huge cracks in the relationship. Taking on these more empowering roles will support both parties in feeling they have won. Each person can feel heard and you can co-create something together.

But I am still stuck

Our focus has been on breaking the patterns of behaviour we become embroiled in during times of stress. What would it be like if you could turn these situations into opportunities to enhance your relationship through deeper understanding? But, desirable as that is, what if you are stuck in the old patterns? Maybe the frequent arguments make change seem impossible. Do you feel reminded of all the hurt and that makes things worse? Emotional pain clouds our ability to see any way out. We end up reliving the pain and become further trapped in fight–flight–freeze survival mode. Please keep your hopes up, there is still another way to resolve this through closure.

Closure: Another Way

If you feel that you're unable to move past your pain, then the chances are that you're holding on to baggage from the past. One of my clients recently said that she didn't want to let go of her baggage just yet, because it would somehow disappear on its own. I asked her how long she'd been holding on to the issue. She said that it had been about five years. Only then did she realize that another five years wouldn't do anything for her, so she had to do something herself. Sometimes releasing our baggage is the only way to gain freedom from our past. Releasing baggage can be the most powerful strategy to regain peace. Only when we feel peace within us can we cultivate it in others. One way of releasing baggage is to bring mercy into the equation. So what is mercy?

Mercy: compassion or forgiveness shown toward someone whom it is within one's power to punish or harm.

Reflect on your pain for a moment. I imagine that it feels raw even now. What is holding on to this pain giving you? Does your pain make the other person suffer? We often hold on to pain as an unconscious attempt to gain justice, or to somehow punish the other person. But, in reality, we are the ones who suffer the most, and the relationship goes up in flames anyway. Imagine that you continue holding on to your pain over the next five, ten, or fifteen years, what impact will this have on your health? On your happiness? On your productivity? On your relationship with this person? Or on your other relationships?

Holding on to the pain keeps us stuck in the past. Our brain always uses past experiences to anticipate what's to come. So, if painful memories are the reference point, this pain will get transferred to other relationships and cause future conflicts and negative patterns in those relationships.

If you want a different result, then you need to start practising mercy. Mercy means to:

- Stop trying to punish or blame.
- Take on one of the roles – coach, creator or supporter we discussed above.
- Truly understand you're not getting anything from holding on to pain.
- Consciously choose a different path of action.

Now there may well be valid reasons why you're holding on to the pain. What may have occurred is still hard to move on from or forgive. That said, look at the cost to you. If you keep holding on to this pain, how will it impact your life ahead? The past is gone, the present is the only time that you have, and the future is unknown. Just keep the next few years in mind, and then make a choice. There may be some lessons that are waiting to be learned. Take some time and ask yourself: what lessons do I need to take from these experiences? Write them down. Then ask yourself: could I allow myself to let go, and be more at peace? Am I willing to give myself better relationships now and in the future? Once you have your answer, you will know what to do.

Letting go can be a difficult and lengthy process. We will explore a simple way to do so.

Exercise 8.4: Releasing The Baggage

Outcome: To support you in gently letting go of any baggage that you're carrying in a relationship.

Method: Follow the steps as laid out.

Step 1: Draw a diagram
Take pen and paper and write down some keywords that represent all the elements that describe this baggage you're holding on to. For example, if you've had a turbulent relationship with a sibling, then think of all the things that represent any past baggage in your relationship with him or her. Words such as "favouritism" "rivalry" "teasing" "arguing" may come up. Allow yourself to brainstorm and be creative. Come up with five or six keywords. Keep it simple.

Step 2: Draw an empty vessel
Now draw something like a hot air balloon, an aircraft, or maybe a ship. You are choosing a mode of transport – something that either flies, floats, or sails away.

Step 3: Draw a loaded vessel
Draw another picture of this vessel with all the baggage loaded on it, ready to be transported. This picture need not be perfect, it just needs to make sense to you.

Step 4: Visualize
Close your eyes. Imagine that you are somewhere peaceful. You can see all these bits of baggage lying there in front of you. Visualize yourself picking up these pieces of baggage and putting them in the vessel. Once you've loaded the cargo, find a way to release the vessel so that it moves away taking all the baggage with it. You can either let the air balloon float away, the ship sail, the plane fly away, or whatever else you imagine. After the baggage has gone, take a moment to absorb feeling free! Notice the open space in front of you and the clear space within. Now open your eyes.

Step 5: Visualize again

Now create a new movie. This is the movie of how you want your relationship with this person to be from now on. See yourself with this person, in a setting where you normally interact (like work or home, etc.). Notice how you interact and the wonderful new relationship you are building. Perhaps you see yourselves spending time together, doing something you both love to do. Enjoy this movie. And allow it to be there in your mind where it needs to be. Then open your eyes.

Releasing any residual baggage will create the emotional space that's necessary to explore new ways of being. If you were unable to work through this chapter effectively, letting go of the baggage may be possible if you are persistent. Go back through the chapter and work through the exercises that now feel most relevant to you.

Let's summarise the main points

Our stress responses interfere with our relationships and our emotional lives in general. We can find ways to handle conflict more effectively, provided we are aware of how we are behaving when we feel threatened. Let's summarise the main points that we talked about in this chapter. We learned that:

- Habits are essentially patterns.
- Stress triggers the fight–flight–freeze mechanism.
- Fight–flight–freeze means we are in survival mode. All creative thinking is shut off.
- When stressed, anything coming at us will feel like a threat, even if it's not meant that way.
- We do have opportunities to break old patterns of conflict and argument.
- We noticed how we react when our buttons get pushed.
- We explored how to break stress-induced behaviour patterns.
- We also noticed that we often fall into the blame game during times of emotional stress.
- We learnt how releasing our own baggage can help create inner peace.

9. Getting Along with Extended Family

Then he is of those who believe and charge one another to show patience, and charge one another to show compassion. These are the people of the right hand.

Qur'an 90:17–18

Kinship is a trial from Allah. Whoever maintains its ties will have ties with Allah, and whoever severs those ties will have them severed by Allah.

Prophet Muhammad (pbuh)

Relationships give joy and cause pain. An argument with a relative or loved one can leave us rattled for days. Relating to others requires vulnerability and effort. However, if we are misunderstood or underappreciated, then it just plain hurts. It can take a long time to heal, and we may never fully forget the pain.

Our feelings are intertwined with our expectations. Feeling misunderstood implies that we expected to be understood. When someone doesn't meet our expectations, we end up feeling disappointed, betrayed or hurt. We discussed expectations in chapter 6 already. However, it needs to be re-emphasized here because we hold expectations towards every person who we regularly interact with. This includes our spouses, children, extended families, and even our communities.

Reflect on your extended family relationships. Does any one person come to mind immediately? Do you have a great relationship, or is it someone you find annoying or hurtful?

Case Study: Rubaab

Rubaab finds it stressful to think about her cousins. She has a big family, who are spread all over the globe. However, the ones who live near her don't treat her very well. She experiences them as stand-offish and rude. She says that she initiated a relationship by being polite and engaging, but after several attempts, she finally chose to give up. She still feels puzzled and hurt by their behaviour. After some coaching, she realized that she had been unable to establish any rapport with them to begin with, so she was able to let her expectation go.

We may pretend that our cousins, aunts, or in-laws don't impact us that much, but these relationships can have a huge impact on our self-esteem.

Are you feeling hurt by a specific relationship in your extended family right now? Would you be willing to do something to make it better? Bear in mind that while certain relationships may be suffering, others might be flourishing. The best way to gain perspective is to gauge your fulfilment in your various extended relationships. First you will need to identify the groups, next measure your fulfilment, and the third step will be to take actions depending on your desired outcomes. The following exercise will help you identify your extended relationships and measure your fulfilment levels for each group.

Exercise 9.1: Identifying Extended Family Relationships

Outcome: To gauge your fulfilment level in various relationships in your life.

Method: Fill in the table and then draw the diagram and fill it in using the instructions and examples that have been laid out below.

Step 1: Identifying extended family relationships
Think about all the important relationships that form your extended family. List even those groups or people you don't see very often. The main point here is to list them according to the impact these groups have on your life directly. Here's an example.

Table 9.1: Distinguishing various relationships

Close relationships (I spend more time with them, interact with them closely and they have an impact on me)	More distant relationships (I spend less time with them, have fewer interactions and they have a lesser impact on me)
Mother-in-law/Father-in-law	Cousins from my mum's side of the family
Brothers-in-law and their families	Mother's brother (my uncle)
Sisters-in-law and their families	
Siblings' families	Extended-in-laws (we only meet once or twice a year)
Father-in-law's brother whom we live with	
Cousins on the WhatsApp group	
Ladies who help in our home (like close family)	

Step 2: Draw the circle diagram in your journal

Draw a circle, and divide it into sections. Allocate each section of the pie to the important relationships, as appropriate. Some sections of the pie could be divided into more than one relationship. For example, the pie for siblings' families could be divided into two or three sections depending on how many siblings (so you make mini slices of the pie); or you could use a separate piece of the pie for each. Also if there are specific people that you would rather focus on from the group, then do that. Divide the pie up in whatever way that feels right to you.

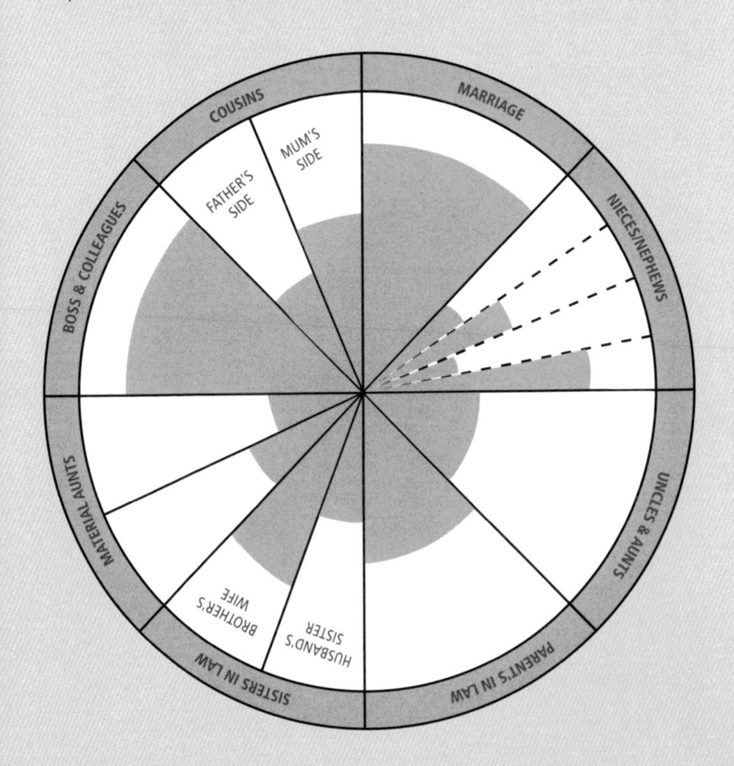

Step 3: Reflect on your extended family relationships

Once you have divided the sections, reflect on one section at a time and ask yourself the following question: "On a scale of 1–10, how fulfilled am I in this particular area or relationship right now?"

Reflect on the number that you sense is coming to you and make a note of it. Then mark this number on the relevant part of the diagram. Consider each piece of the pie as representing the scale, with the outside most part of the circle being "10" and the centre being "1". Make an arc inside the pie slice at the relevant number. Essentially, you will be making a wheel inside the wheel. Go through the entire pie till you have got all the areas mapped out. If a section or two remains empty, do not be concerned. If something occurs to you, you can always fill It in later.

Step 4: Gauging your fulfilment

Address one relationship at a time and ask yourself the following questions. If you have several relationships in one section, then by all means choose the most important one, and start there. Make sure to note your answers as you go along.

- What do I see, feel, and experience in this relationship area that tells me that I'm at this number?
- What's working in this relationship?
- What's not working in this relationship?
- What am I doing or saying that might be causing or contributing to the issues we are experiencing?
- How might I respond differently?

Now that you've begun reflecting on your extended relationships, you may have a good idea of which ones really enrich your life, while noticing the ones that are an energy drain. Remember, you can never change your mother-in-law, your boss, or the gossipy lady at the mosque, but you can change your responses to their behaviour. The other person's behaviour may not shift, but the quality of your life will improve.

Relationships are about meeting needs

Let's remind ourselves of the concept that people maintain relationships to fulfil needs. People's behaviours indicate what's happening for them at a deeper level. Consider, that if someone is acting in an aggressive or distant way, they have an unfulfilled need that they perceive should be met by you. If we are behaving negatively towards someone, perhaps we need to explore what's motivating our behaviour. It often seems that we are upset because of something the other person said or did, but a period of prolonged upset shows up when a relationship is not meeting the needs that we associate with it.

So, if one or more of your extended relationships isn't working, there may be an opportunity to explore what you're really feeling. Which need is not being met? Explore through the short exercise below.

Exercise 9.2: Exploring Our Needs

Outcome: To explore what's provoking your negative behaviours in specific relationships.

Method: Look at the circle diagram from the previous exercise, then follow the steps below:

Step 1: Examine your diagram and note the relationships that aren't working well.

Step 2: Work through one relationship at a time, filling in the table below. Use the example as a guide. The aim here is to learn about your own needs.

Table 9.2: Learning about my own needs

Relationship that is not working (note the number on the fulfilment scale)	What is the issue?	How am I currently acting? What am I doing, or saying?	What could be the reason for my behaving this way?	What need is not being met?
Mother-in-law (4/10)	She complains to my husband about me, behind my back.	I was very open before. Now, I am not interacting much. I just reply when she asks me something. I do as she asks. Keeping my distance, being withholding.	I feel hurt and sad. I want to protect myself. Prevent arguments between my spouse and myself.	The need to feel safe. The need to be able to trust her. The need for support.
My aunt (3/10)	Constant interference. She complains to my mother about me – behind my back.	I yelled at her last week. It was a showdown.	I am very angry. I am not sure at whom: my mother, or her.	My significance with my mom. I want to feel important, valued, like I matter. I feel that my aunt is more important to my mother than I am.
My Boss (4/10)	She is always watching everything I do. Changing targets at the last minute.	I can't say anything. I am taking all my holidays in one go.	I am afraid she will fire me. I am trying to avoid a confrontation.	I am not being heard. This job is doable as it is.

What did you learn from the previous exploration? What are you noticing about your own behaviour? It's not uncommon to blame the other person entirely, but let's remember that we play a part in the relationship too. Now is the time to increase your awareness, so you can notice what's going on at a deeper level.

Why does this relationship feel so bad?

Okay, so you're not being your best self in certain relationships, but you do intend to improve them, so that's a huge step right there. And what if you've already been trying, but the relationship still doesn't work. You're doing what you think they want, yet things are as bad as before. This can feel very hopeless or frustrating.

Frustration may not be the only emotion at play. Do you feel obligated, afraid, or guilty about giving in? Are you feeling sorry for them? Are you afraid how they might react if you say no? Are you just giving in, while feeling upset and resentful underneath? Maybe the resentment is showing up indirectly. We all compromise at times, but giving in to pressure on a regular basis indicates that there may be a more serious issue underneath. Consistently perceiving pressure to give in may indicate that you're feeling emotionally blackmailed. So how do you know if you're reacting to emotional blackmail? Let's define it.

Emotional blackmail is any strategy that has you giving in to another person's demand, not because you want to but because you feel that you have to.

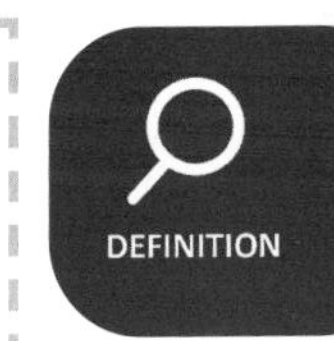

Let's take a hypothetical story to understand this concept a little bit better. Imagine that a Muslim family has a daughter studying at college abroad. While visiting home on holiday, she announces that she likes someone and wants to marry him. He isn't Muslim, but is willing to convert. He is also a different race, has a different financial background and upbringing. The girl is telling her parents about him, and they listen to her quietly. After she is finished, the father tells his daughter that if she goes ahead with it, they will disinherit her. She will be dead to them and so on. She's brought shame on them and their family, and they cannot tolerate this under any circumstances. She must choose between her parents and the boy.

This type of example isn't entirely unheard of, is it? Would it be considered emotional blackmail? Yes, definitely. This is because the girl has been put in a very difficult position. This is not just a demand, but a demand with very heavy strings attached. She must choose between two things that are equally important to her – her family and someone she wants to marry. The double jeopardy for her is either losing her parents or losing her love.

Just imagine how this girl must feel. Her parents might be acting out of a sense of fear or protective love, but that's the last thing she would feel. She feels stuck between a rock and a hard place. She feels her needs don't matter to her parents, and that she doesn't matter. She feels blackmailed by their ultimatum. She feels threatened by the loss of her family and by the promise to disinherit her.

Putting pressure on someone to do something while implying a loss if they don't comply is emotionally blackmailing them.

Is making a demand always a bad thing?

A demand is when you express an important need that you **must** have met. If you were making a request, the person asked has a choice of saying yes or no. However, when a demand is made, the implication is that it must be fulfilled.

Having said that, making a demand isn't always a bad thing. We all make demands from the people we are close to. Think about when you've asked for something from someone close. You said it very nicely, trying not to impose, but the other person knew that it was something you definitely needed. Having a need or making a demand, doesn't mean that you're necessarily blackmailing someone. ***Blackmail isn't the demand itself, but the strategy used to make it.*** If someone just asked us for something in a straightforward way, without any drama, then we will probably do it, or may feel okay to say yes or no. We would know that it's okay for us to refuse. However, a demand will feel like blackmail when it's emotionally charged. The demand is made in such a way that the other person feels forced to give in, because they're going to lose something important if they don't. They are either made to feel afraid, guilty or obligated. The tone may be subtle, but the request has strings attached. The person experiencing this gives in because they feel compelled to avoid the potential loss they're being blackmailed with. For example:

- Not being able to see the kids (fear of losing a loved one).
- A parent's disapproval (strong obligation towards them).
- Punishment of some sort (silent treatment, taking away something).
- Risking a job or a promotion (losing something one's working towards).
- Looking like a failure or loser in front of the community (fear of losing face).
- Financial privileges being taken away (loss of security).
- Bringing shame on the family (guilt/obligation to family).

For now, let's summarize two main points. The first point is that blackmail is a demand with "strings attached". The second point is that there's an experience of pressure to give into that demand because the cost of refusal is too high. The person being blackmailed isn't being given the freedom to say no.

Please remember that it's natural for people to hold expectations and make demands in their relationships. In most relationships, both parties give and take, although not necessarily equally, but the principle of exchange is there. *Emotional blackmail exists in a relationship where the principle of exchange, of give and take, has stopped or become skewed.* The relationship has become one-sided. The most important point here is that the person giving in is feeling pressured to do so! Many of us give more at some time or another, and we do it happily because we care. However, if there's a feeling this isn't quite right, then we know that something is off-balance, deep down. We may not call it blackmail as, after all, that's a very harsh term, but we know that something is off.

So now that we understand that *pressure is a symptom* of emotional blackmail, let's explore this concept further. Why do we feel pressure in the first place? After all, someone close to us is just trying to convince us to do something. If we explore the situation objectively, we would probably remind ourselves that the person may not even follow through on the so-called threat. Yet, the minute we hear it, we sense deep and imminent danger that compels us to give in. This sense of danger is a big deal. Our mind–body system is designed to protect us, so we will naturally react to any threat.

Human beings are innately driven to flee painful and threatening situations towards safety. As discussed in chapter 8, the mind–body system cannot distinguish between real and imagined threats. **Human beings naturally tend to move towards pleasure, and away from pain. This driving force is at the core of our behaviour, and the decisions we make.**

This need explains why we are drawn towards or run away from certain people and situations. Blackmail is effective because it works along this principle. The person being blackmailed is either being presented with the possibility of something amazing happening, or the dread that some serious loss may occur. The two don't always occur together, so therefore we can place emotional blackmail into two main categories.

Category 1: If you do/don't do this, then something bad will happen

This is when a person is pressured into believing that their doing, or not doing something will lead to some type of punishment, harm or loss. The harm can be physical, mental, financial or emotional in nature. For example:

Table 9.3: Exploring emotional blackmail in category 1

Category 1	What he/ she may say	What he or she may be doing
The blackmailer hurting him/ herself.	How will I manage? I will just die without you. I will get sick and it will be all your fault.	Calling several times. Drama. Long emotional texts or emails.
The black-mailed will experience some harm.	We will deny access to the kids and you won't see them again. I will disinherit you. You won't get any monthly allowance. You will lose this promo-tion if… "We are not speaking until you" …. "you're useless, worthless, you're an idiot" (name calling). Do you want me to hit you? I'm going to take away your phone, and your privileges.	Silent treatment. Cutting off monthly allowance. Complaining to third parties. Yelling, name calling, threatening. Taking things away.

Category 2: If you do/don't do this, then we can't have that

This category of emotional blackmail relates to our basic human need to feel good. This type of emotional blackmail occurs when a person is being pressured to do or not do something in order to achieve a certain dream. The blackmailer presents it in such a way that doing or not doing a certain thing will impact the result.

Table 9.4: Exploring emotional blackmail in category 2

Category 2: The promise of the dream. What is the dream?	What the blackmailer may say	What the blackmailer may be doing
A promise of a marriage/life together.	You are the one I love.	Having an extra-marital affair.
	I don't love her anymore.	Promising to leave his spouse.
	We will have a wonderful life together.	
A new home/ car/ something for the lifestyle.	You can ask your parents to help. That's the only way we can afford it, it is for you after all.	Pressuring the person to ask family for financial help (coercion).
	You have some money saved up. Can't you do this for us?	Pressuring the other person to use their money for this thing they both want.
A new promotion.	If you put in these extra hours, it puts you in the running.	Dumping his or her work on the other person.

Reflect on the time when someone in your life kept promising you a reward that never came. How did that feel? The person kept making promises, but never delivered. Or perhaps you got roped into doing all the work – you did it because you were invested in the dream but felt resentful the entire time.

One common example that I've seen is with young people who are in school or college. A group of kids get together to work on a project. A couple of kids are laid back and don't do anything, while the others do all the work and feel resentful about it. They often keep quiet because the other people are "friends". This "freeloader" phenomenon is a very common situation where some people do the work to keep the boat afloat, while others just hitch a free ride without making any effort.

Another common scenario happens in group dynamics. One person bends over backwards to get others to like him or her, while the others feel free to leave him or her out of various social interactions. The person keeps trying to fit in, but somehow never feels that s/he does.

Please note that if blackmail turns into abuse of any sort, then it's time to get some intervention, and perhaps make a decision to end that relationship. Self-preservation is key. We are only discussing emotional blackmail here, which is, to be honest, quite common (rather than the much rarer criminal blackmail that involves extortion, kidnapping or threat of violence). People often fall into patterns of giving in to the pressures of emotional blackmail without even realizing it. For example, if a lady was treated a certain way by her in-laws, she may be replicating the same thing with her daughter-in-law as default behaviour – not because she's malicious, but because it's what she knows.

We all bring our own patterns and baggage into relationships. The very first step is to identify and understand what's happening in your situation so you can make a change for the better. Look at the example on the next page, and explore if you can relate to it.

You may now have an inkling whether emotional blackmail is present in one of your extended family relationships. However, before jumping to any firm conclusion, it's important to differentiate between what's real and what's imagined. Go ahead and work on the exercise.

Exercise 9.3: Differentiating The Fear From The Facts:

Desired outcome: To gain clarity on the actual event that occurred, the demand, while separating the emotions from the event.

Method: Answer the question, and fill in the table below.

Step 1: Think about a situation where you feel there might be some blackmail going on. This can be an ongoing situation, or something that happens on different occasions, but with a similar pattern. Write down the (most recent) event in terms of what exactly occurred. Think about the demand that was/is being made. Reflect on the pressure that you're feeling. What is the potential dream, or threat?

Step 2: Draw a table and fill it in.

Table 9.5: Exploring the dynamics of the demand being made

Draw a table in your coaching notebook using the guidelines in the diagram. The example is just to help you get started. Aim to keep your answers to the point. Remember, this is to give you clarity on the situation.

Follow the pattern of the table and make one from your own experience of emotional blackmail.

What actually happened (the facts). The event.	What is the demand being made?	What is the dream or the threat? What is the pressure that I am feeling? What might be taken away if I don't do this? Or what may I not get, if I do/ don't do this?	How did I react to? the demand? To any pressure that was there? What did I end up doing/ not doing?
My mother-in-law comes over every weekend. This weekend, we had to visit my family, and we had accepted the invite a few weeks ago, so I told her that we are busy. She called my husband and talked to him. My husband called me, and yelled at me.	That we spend every weekend with my mother-in-law. Either we go to her, or she comes to our home.	I feel the pressure that my husband will get upset, we will have an argument, or he will leave. I fear my marriage will end.	I yelled back. I defended myself to my husband. I went to my family event alone, which felt awful. I didn't give in but felt very guilty after that.

Step 3: How might I react differently the next time I feel the pressure? What might I do or not do differently?

Situations teach us a lot about ourselves

Did you notice the demand? Were you able to decipher what the threat was? If you noticed your specific response to stress or pressure, then you've made wonderful progress. Whatever your specific behaviour, know that everyone's behaviour and reactions develop as coping strategies for self-preservation. We all go through difficulties, and our unconscious mind works hard for survival. This is true for both sides in these sorts of situations that hold a promise and/or threat.

This knowledge is very handy. It teaches you that the person pressuring you is not evil or mean; rather, it's likely that this is how he or she copes when things don't go according to expectations. He or she is trying to meet a need. The issue is that you are also trying to meet your needs as well. The most important thing now is to focus on your own awareness first. Learn about your own boundaries so you can then choose a different way to respond the next time they're being crossed.

How do I see the demands?

Every relationship has its demands. The boss wants the work done. Kids have their own needs. Friends want time and support. Again, this is not a bad thing in itself – we make demands of our own too. However, there are different categories of demands. Some demands are inconvenient but won't impact us emotionally. Others impact our sense of self-worth. So let's explore how we can divide them up.

Let's divide demands into three main categories

I've divided demands into various categories depending on their emotional impact. When we think of a demand being a "big deal", it means that it has a heavy emotional impact on how you see the situation and yourself. All demands require some physical effort, but not all of them will impact your emotional wellbeing in a detrimental way.

1. It's something small. This type of demand is asking for an everyday need to be fulfilled. It will require some effort, but is not a big deal emotionally. For example:

- Having lunch with the in-laws once a week.
- Creating home-cooked meals, or keeping the home tidy.
- Accompanying your spouse on a business dinner with his/her work colleagues.
- Buying gifts for extended family when on holiday.
- Taking your father-in-law to the doctor.

2. A demand involving an important issue. These are demands regarding issues that matter to you. These demands impact important decisions, and are a big deal, but they don't intend to compromise your core values or self-worth. They do, however, impact you emotionally as they require a life change, possibly a big compromise.

- Financial decisions such as who works, managing child care, where to go on holiday, or home renovations.Demands on each other's spare time.
- Having the in-laws move in.

3. A demand where the stakes are too high. These are demands where your integrity, or self-esteem are impacted. Giving into this demand would mean that you're giving up on your core values. For example:

- Being forced to stay silent or lie when you know the other person is doing something wrong.
- Being asked/ told how to dress, but it doesn't feel right to you.
- Demands on changing your personal life choices (could be important things like praying, alcohol use, social interactions).
- Demands around religious practices/ teaching the kids, etc.
- To do something that feels dangerous in any way.
- Being in a situation that compromises your physical, mental, or emotional health.

We don't often think about demands in this way, because life moves at too fast a pace. In situations where we feel pressured, we give in to keep the peace, but on reflection realize it wasn't a good idea. You have a unique set of circumstances so the demands being made are particular to you. The three categories allow you to explore what sorts of demands are being made on you and where you stand with them. They allow you to think more clearly about your own boundaries when it comes to responding to the demands made upon you. Now is the time to be clear about when you can be flexible, and where you know you cannot give in. Ask yourself the following questions through the exercise below.

Exercise 9.4: Defining My Boundaries

Outcome: To explore your own boundaries regarding various demands in your life.

Step 1: How are your boundaries being challenged?
Reflect on the relationship that's challenging you currently. Bring the other person to mind (whether it's a friend, boss, or family member). Close your eyes and think about the last time you felt uncomfortable or pressurized by this person's demands.
Replay this event in your mind as if you are watching a movie of it. Play the event from start to finish and then open your eyes.

When you have finished watching the movie. Get up, give yourself a good shake or walk around for a while. Then sit down in a different spot. Please make sure to do this, because you now need to sit in a neutral space.

Step 2: Begin to take notes in your notebook

- Make a list of the demands you noticed.
- Notice which category the demands belong to.
- Notice how you handled the situation.

Step 3: Reflect on your boundaries
Fill in the table below as appropriate. I have just given you examples in every category, but you may be dealing with just one. Focus on what comes up for you.

Table 9.6: Reflecting on my boundaries

Category	The demands	Where I am flexible	These are my red lines
It's life – not such a big deal	Take mum-in-law to doctors. Have extended family stay 2x per year. Cook fresh food daily. Manage the groceries within the budget given.	I can take mum-in-law, but only when its planned. I will do the groceries.	I don't have the time to cook fresh food every meal. (We need to find a compromise.) Extended family – once a year max. The other time is for us.
Demands involving an important issue	If I want to go on holiday – I should pay for it.	I can save little by little.	If my spouse wants to come, s/he needs to contribute.
Stakes are too high – this is about my self-esteem, my integrity, my core values	My spouse wants that friends should be able to bring alcohol when we entertain them – I don't drink and I know he doesn't either, but they should be able to.		No, no and no! If he wants to hang out with them, it will have to be outside. And I will not come.

Step 4: Further reflection

Think about the questions below.

- From the demands being made of me, which ones am I willing to compromise on?
- If demand seems like emotional blackmail, what am I now willing to say about it?
- What, if any, personal boundaries are being crossed? What are things that I can't compromise on at all?
- Am I willing to end the relationship because this boundary is being crossed?
- Where might I be pressurizing the other person? Am I willing to stop? How do I stop myself from this?

Making things better

These explorations make one realize the people we demonize aren't evil – they're just human beings trying their best. We go through challenges and react or respond in our own unique ways. Most people look to survive and thrive in life the best way that they can. Think about some of the challenges that this so-called emotional blackmailer has faced. Maybe you know about some of them. Imagine how difficult those challenges may have been. Appreciating that we all have a unique model of the world is so handy. With this awareness, we can think of the other person as human too, which makes our work to improve the relationship so much easier, doesn't it? Now let's look at a few practical strategies that can help us along in our journey.

Strategy 1: Calm and neutral responses

Do you tend to be defensive when you're feeling pressured? That the more defensive you were, the more the pressure increased? Apologizing, negotiating or defending often doesn't work in emotionally charged interactions. Breaking away from such charged interactions is often difficult and even impossible *during* the interaction. If anything is to change, one person must have a greater awareness and do something different.

One very effective strategy is to use neutral and calm language. Imagine if someone is pressuring you, but you're able to remain calm. How might that impact the situation? It would probably diffuse the situation. Using neutral language is a technique to calm down a volatile situation while calmly setting a personal boundary. The other person gets the message that their behaviour is unacceptable, and you get to communicate it in such a way that deescalates the situation. Before we discuss neutral language further, let's explore how we normally communicate. Reflect on a recent interaction where the situation escalated. What do you remember doing? Were you?

- Apologizing repeatedly.
- Yelling and shouting.
- Defending yourself.
- Kept asking what was wrong.

How did you feel during the interaction? Did you feel in control? Did those strategies work? Most likely they didn't. The above types of communication give the message that we believe that we somehow caused the escalation or that we are wrong to set a boundary or just say no. In turn, this adds to the pressure and the situation often escalates. With using neutral and calm language, you deescalate the situation *and* show that emotional blackmail is unacceptable to you. Reflect on your relationships and come up with some examples. Look at the following as a guide.

- Let's talk later (if things are getting heated).
- I sense that you're upset about this (you're not taking all the blame, you are empathizing).
- I know you're very angry right now.
- Yelling won't resolve this, let's talk when you are calmer.

Now come up with a few expressions of your own. Write them down and begin to practise them.

I know de-escalating is important, but I need to express my needs too

Okay, so you're getting better at dealing with the fear, guilt or pressure in the moment. But this hasn't solved the problem. You still have needs of your own to express, and you're not sure how to do that. What would it be like to be able to say your piece calmly? Would it be good if the fear or feelings of obligation didn't overwhelm you? The only way to do this is to be aware of what comes up, and to practise how you might handle it. You may not control the outcome, but you'd be expressing yourself without doling out blame. Here's a strategy to do just that.

Strategy 2: Practise the Response

1. Take time out and be clear about what you have to say. This is about your own boundaries and needs.
2. Explore what the other person may say, so that you can consider your response carefully.
3. Communicate clearly and simply.

The following exercise is designed to help you practice:

Exercise 9.5: Communicating My Boundaries

Outcome: To practise communicating your own needs.

Method: Go through the steps below.

Step 1: Clarity
Go back to the list you made earlier. Keeping this in front of you, think about the demand that you need to set a boundary for. This is something you need to communicate but have been unable to do so due to fear or unclear communication. List what you are now going to do/ not do.

Example: "I am going back to work because i need financial freedom."

Take the time to review and your words so that you express your need in the most clear and straightforward way. Remember you want to come across as clearly as possible – so the other person can immediately understand what you mean. You are also getting clarity on what you want, and that may take some exploration. It may take a few attempts to find that clarity but give yourself the time to get there.

Step 2: Preparing my response
Clearly you know the other person, so you can predict how they are likely to respond. You have now resolved to communicate your needs. This is the time to practise your response to any objections or reactions they may have. Reflect on what you need to say, and how you can communicate that as calmly and clearly as possible. Use the example below and create your own list of responses.

Table 9.7: Exploring possible responses

What he or she may say	How I will respond
"You are bringing shame on the family; how can you do this?"	"I do love you all. But I need to do what's right for me." "I know that you love me."
"I'm trying to do something for your future. How can you be so selfish and not see that?"	"I can see that you are upset. I would like to tell you how I came to this decision." "I know you are angry right now, but I hope, that in time, you may reconsider if you keep an open mind."
"We won't ever talk again."	"That is of your choice of course. I will always love you and want you to be part of my life." "I do hope that when you calm down, you will reconsider."

Step 3: Practise
This step is extremely important. You can practise your speech by yourself, or ask someone to help you through role playing. If you are feeling nervous, then you can practise your lines in advance to give you confidence. You will also get the opportunity to readjust what you're going to say, if need be. Take all the time you need.

Step 4: Plan to meet and have the conversation

Find a time and place that suits both parties and schedule a time when you both can be relaxed. Remember to keep things as calm and neutral as possible. Make sure to avoid any blame. Just do your best and leave the rest up to Allah swt, as He has the ultimate say in the outcome!

Step 5: Observations

Once you have completed your conversation, take some time later on to reflect on it. How did it go? How did the other person receive your communication? How was your behaviour? Did you stay calm? Give the other person some time to reflect on your position. He or she will come back to you when ready. Or you will know by their behaviour whether they have accepted your message or not.

Some tips to keep in mind

Communicating our needs may not be easy, especially if we aren't used to doing so. Here are some basic dos and don'ts that may help.

Dos

- Do listen – reflect on whether it's a legitimate need being asked of you.
- Do take accountability for your behaviour and your choices.
- Do stick to the issue.
- Do be willing to find a solution.
- Do let some things go.

Don'ts

- Don't blame the other person for being unreasonable.
- Don't retaliate or try to take revenge.
- Don't escalate the situation.
- Don't be unyielding if there's room for negotiation.

What if there's no clear-cut solution?

Some demands will feel like an all-or-nothing situation. You may also be in a position where you can't compromise at all. Still, do also consider the impact of a stalemate. If this is a relationship that needs to or you want it to remain in your life, then what would be the better alternative?

Remember that both parties are just trying to meet their needs. So wouldn't it be better to carve out a solution, rather than being stuck at polar opposites? What if you worked with the other person, and included them in the process? The chances are that when the emotional blackmailer sees you are open to working with them, they might work with you. A productive way of moving forward is to look for a win-win solution. Ask the other person to think about what they need, and you do the same.

Next, explore what a "win" would look like for each of you. It may not be exactly what each of you wants, but it will include a big part of what you were aiming for.

Sit down and discuss the win-win solution together. Then come to an agreement where each of you makes a commitment. If you like, write it down. Also agree on a date when you will reassess the arrangement. This agreement will give you a productive way forward. *Insha'Allah*, the relationship will find a firmer footing with time.

Last but not least forgive

Human beings are strange in how flexible they are. You have done so much work through the exercises. I'm sure you've raised your awareness around the other person's humanity and your own. *Insha'Allah*, these strategies will continue to work for you. However, do keep one essential thing in mind. Any resentments from the past can play havoc with your efforts in the present. If you are looking to create lasting change in a relationship, then forgiveness can give you access to truly making this happen. Releasing past resentments will allow you to "see" the person in a new light and create a more fulfilling present and future. Find a way that works for you, let go of the past, and leave the possibility of a more beautiful relationship to remain open.

Let's summarize the main points

- We carved out the important extended relationships.
- Explored our fulfilment levels in these relationships.
- Emphasized that each relationship has needs.
- We learned that emotional blackmail occurs if we are feeling pressured to give in to someone's demands while not being truly willing to.
- We explored what someone's demands may be.
- We worked on defining our own boundaries.
- We learned strategies to communicate our own position.
- We learned that the other person isn't necessarily bad. They are just human trying to meet their needs like we are.
- We explored the possibility of creating a win-win solution.
- We ended with the reminder that forgiveness helps us keep possibilities for a better relationship alive.

Resources and Recommended Reading

Here are some resources that I have used for research in this book. They are wonderful resources if you would like to explore any of the themes raised in the book, or for general interest.

Chapman, Gary D., *The 5 Love Languages: The Secret to Love that Lasts. (USA Northfield Publishing. 2010).* (Please note that this book contains Biblical references.)

Forward, Susan, *Emotional Blackmail: When the People in Your Life use Fear, Obligation and Guilt to Manipulate You* (USA: HarperCollins Publishers, 1997).

Harley, Jr., Willard F., *His Needs, Her Needs: Building an Affair-Proof Marriage* (Grand Rapids, MI: Fleming H. Randell, YEAR), Ch. 2. This is what I based the idea of the "Relationship Reserve" on. (Please note that this book contains Biblical references.)

McCready, Amy, www.positiveparentingsolutions.com. This is a wonderful online parenting course.

McKenna, Paul, and Hugh Willbourn, *How to Mend Your Broken Heart* (London: Transworld Publishers, 2003). For more on the anchor technique see page 96; for more on developing positive intentions see pages 65–9.

Index